Problem-based Learning in Higher Education: Untold Stories

Problem-based Learning in Higher Education: Untold Stories

Maggi Savin-Baden

The Society for Research into Higher Education
& Open University Press

Published by SRHE and
Open University Press
Celtic Court
22 Ballmoor
Buckingham
MK18 1XW

email: enquiries@openup.co.uk
worldwide web: www.openup.co.uk

and 325 Chestnut Street
Philadelphia, PA 19106, USA

First published 2000
Reprinted 2000

A catalogue record of this book is available from the British Library.

ISBN 0 335 20338 8 (hb)   0 335 20337 X (pb)

Library of Congress Cataloging-in-Publication Data
Savin-Baden, Maggi, 1960–
    Problem-based learning in higher education: untold stories /
Maggi Savin-Baden.
        p.   cm.
    Includes bibliographical references (p.) and index.
    ISBN 0-335-20338-8 (hardbound). — ISBN 0-335-20337-X (pbk.)
    1. Problem-based learning.   2. Education, Higher.   3. Adult
learning.   I. Title.
LB1027.42.S28   2000
378.1'7—dc21   99-41043
                                                             CIP

Typeset by Graphicraft Limited, Hong Kong
Printed in Great Britain by St Edmundsbury Press, Bury St Edmunds, Suffolk

For John, with love and thanks

Contents

Acknowledgements

I would like to thank Ron Barnett for his mentorship and in particular for the invaluable advice he provided during the process of undertaking this venture. I would equally like to thank Susan Weil who has been a constant source of encouragement, always challenging me to push my own boundaries and to explore my own untold stories.

There have been many critical friends who commented on the manuscript at various points and my thanks are due in particular to: Auldeen Alsop, Jean Barr, David Cormack, Della Freeth, John Skelton and my parents Joyce and Frank Savin. I am also grateful to all those who have participated in my research, agreed to be quoted here and also to those who continue to be part of my current work.

Finally, thanks are due to John Savin-Baden for his support, patience, proof-reading, salient comments and his critical sense of humour. The views expressed here and any errors are mine.

Prologue

It is Monday morning, 8.45, and the door of the design studio bursts open. Tim and Bill rush over to Jack to tell him that they have cracked the problem scenario. The group have been working on the problem all weekend but struggled, until now, to figure it out. The two who have found a way of managing the problem scenario share their views with the others. The group is oblivious to the tutor until he comes over to tell them that they have got the wrong answer. They are defeated, deflated and distraught that they have worked so hard for no result. Tim remains unconvinced that they are wrong and while the tutor gives the class a mini lecture he sits and works it all out again. At the end of the session, the group argue with the tutor who discovers, through this group, that there are in fact several ways to solve this particular problem.

One of the difficulties today is in writing a book that reflects the complexity of its subject. The students in the scenario above demonstrate some of the challenges for staff and students involved with programmes that use problem-based learning. For example, part of the challenge for the students here was in being prepared to contest the solution proffered by the tutor; to value their own perspectives and their own voices enough in the learning process to argue their case. Being able to do this is something that many students who have previously experienced lecture-based methods of learning at school or at college will find complex and difficult. This is because problem-based learning demands of them a sound understanding of the knowledge they have researched and explored, and an ability to critique information. At the same time they are also expected to take up a position towards the problem situation with which they have been presented in relation both to their prior experience and the new knowledge they have gained. Problem-based learning can offer students opportunities to engage *with* complexity, and help them both to see ambiguity and learn to manage the ambiguities that prevail in professional life. It can also help students to integrate learning across subjects and disciplines and to take up a position towards the knowledge on offer. For staff, the challenges of using problem-based learning are equally complex in that they relate not only to issues of teaching and learning; but also to the personal challenges that emerge as students question their perspectives and prior experience.

Making sense of problem-based learning

Problem-based learning is an approach to learning that has grown in breadth and depth across the world since the 1970s, yet the bulk of the literature concentrates on practical applications of problem-based learning in particular settings rather than on the examination of the complexities and challenges involved in its application. This book sets out to challenge some of the current understandings of problem-based learning (which have largely emerged through misconceptions of problem-based learning as a complex and multi-faceted approach to learning) through setting up the argument that the potential of problem-based learning is yet to be fully realized. This argument stems from a number of perspectives. First, as a researcher I saw, and continue to see, problem-based learning implemented in diverse curricula and what is apparent is that problem-based learning can help students to 'make sense' for themselves. What I mean here is that problem-based learning is an approach to learning through which many students have been enabled to understand their own situations and frameworks so that they are able to perceive how they learn, and how they see themselves as future professionals. Yet in many curricula these issues are not often fully acknowledged, nor are students supported in managing the personal and learning challenges with which they are presented through problem-based learning. Research findings will be used to demonstrate and support this argument in the form of a framework, termed Dimensions of Learner Experience, which emerged *from* data that arose out of the first British cross-site study into problem-based learning (Savin-Baden, 1996). This study explored staff and students' expectations and experiences of problem-based learning in four different professions and educational environments.

Second, the argument has emerged from my own fascination about the ways in which the theory of problem-based learning is (and is not) played out in practice. For example, there is a confusion about the difference between problem-based learning and problem-solving learning. Problem-solving learning is the type of teaching many staff have been using for years and the focus is upon giving students a lecture or an article to read and then a set of questions based upon the information given. Students are expected to find the solutions to these answers and bring them to a seminar as a focus for discussion. Problem scenarios here are set within and bounded by a discrete subject or disciplinary area. In some curricula students are given specific training in problem-solving techniques, but in many cases they are not. The focus in this kind of learning is largely on acquiring the answers expected by the lecturer, answers that are rooted in the information supplied in some way to the students. Thus, the solutions are always linked to a specific curricula content, which is seen as vital for students to cover in order for them to be competent and effective practitioners. The solutions are therefore bounded by the content and students are expected to explore little extra material other than that provided in order to discover the solutions.

Problem-based learning is different. The focus here is in organizing the curricular content around problem scenarios rather than subjects or disciplines. Students work in groups or teams to solve or manage these situations but they are not expected to acquire a predetermined series of 'right answers'. Instead they are expected to engage with the complex situation presented to them and decide what information they need to learn and what skills they need to gain in order to manage the situation effectively. There are many different ways of implementing problem-based learning but the underlying philosophies associated with it as an approach are broadly more student-centred than those underpinning problem-solving learning. This is because students are offered opportunities, through problem-based learning, to explore a wide range of information, to link the learning with their own needs as learners and to develop independence in enquiry. Problem-based learning is thus an approach to learning that is characterized by flexibility and diversity in the sense that it can be implemented in a variety of ways in and across different subjects and disciplines in diverse contexts. As such it can therefore look very different to different people at different times depending on the staff and students involved in the programmes utilizing it. However, what will be similar will be the focus of learning around problem scenarios rather than discrete subjects.

It is possible to trace the origins of problem-based learning back to early forms of learning that demanded the diverse kinds of problem-solving and problem management that emerge in problem-based curricula. For example, Socrates presented students with problems that through questioning enabled him to help them explore their assumptions, their values and the inadequacies of their proffered solutions. Aristotle, too, argued that in 'every area' the philosopher, or in our case, the student, has got to begin by setting down what he terms 'the appearances'. Thus, in working on a particular problem, say for example the problem of knowledge, the philosopher would begin by setting down the 'appearances' of knowledge. What would be included under this heading would not just be our perceptual experiences but also our ordinary beliefs about knowledge. Having set this down the philosopher will look for any contradictions. If contradictions are found, sifting and sorting will occur until decisions are made about which beliefs are more central than others and these will be preserved, others that conflict will be discarded, and so in the end it will be possible to return to ordinary discourse with increased understanding. This kind of increased understanding and examination of perspectives and frameworks is encouraged through problem-based learning because it offers students opportunities to examine their beliefs about knowledge in ways that lecture-based learning and narrow forms of problem-solving learning do not.

More recently the work of Dewey (1938) has influenced the way in which knowledge is perceived: not as something that is reliable and changeless but as something that is an *activity*, a process of finding out. Dewey's challenge to the world of science – that *we* are the very stuff and substance of the world and as such we must work from the middle of a situation in which our most reliable beliefs are at best imperfect or inadequate – is that we are not spectators, but agents of change. Dewey's perspective was thus a pragmatic stance towards knowledge. He argued that knowledge was bound up with activity and thus he opposed theories of knowledge that considered knowledge to be independent of its role in problem-solving enquiry. His views on this were played out in practice by his emphasis on learning by doing, which can be seen as essentially a problem-solving approach to learning. The fact that much of what Dewey proposed is now largely taken for granted in many areas of higher and professional education can perhaps be said to be a measure of his success.

Although it has been argued here that learning through exploring problem situations is not new (this will be addressed further in Chapter 1) problem-based learning was popularized during the 1960s as a result of research by Barrows (Barrows and Tamblyn, 1980) into the reasoning abilities of medical students. Their research stemmed from a desire to develop in medical students the ability to relate the knowledge they had gained to the problems with which the patients presented, something they found that few medical students could do well. Yet when Barrows and Tamblyn undertook their study, which in many ways could be said to have alerted the world of higher education to problem-based learning, they probably had little real understanding of the worldwide impact it would still be having decades later. What they highlighted were clear differences between problem-solving learning and learning in ways that used problem scenarios to encourage students to engage themselves in the learning process; problem-based learning. Yet the attraction of problem-based learning and its uptake during the 1970s and 1980s in Canada, Australia and the United States, and during the late 1980s in the UK, seemed to lie not only in its timely emergence in relation to other worldwide changes in higher education, but also because of new debates about professional education. These related to a growing recognition that there needed to be not just a different view of learning and professional education, but also a different view about relationships between industry and education, between learning and society and between government and universities. Such debates continue. For example, the shifts away from the relatively unfashionable notion of liberal education, that is the kind of education where students are encouraged to have virtually unrestricted access to knowledge and that knowledge is to be valued for its own sake, have meant shifts towards curricula that focus on what students are able to *do*. These kinds of curricula I shall term operational curricula (after Barnett, 1994) since they tend to focus on encouraging students to develop narrow sets of prestated competencies. By focusing curricula upon such narrow skills students are consequently offered little scope or latitude in terms of the long-term usefulness of such sets of skills to professional life. Yet the kind of higher education that can help develop in students the capacities to be able to operate effectively in society, whilst simultaneously giving them opportunities to have unrestricted access to knowledge, is on offer through problem-based learning. Problem-based learning is an approach that can embrace both liberal education and operational curricula, by offering students opportunities for undertaking learning that holds real meaning for them in circumstances where knowledge is valued for its own sake *as well as* in the context of accountability and market related values.

Finally, the argument that problem-based learning is yet to be realized developed from my own frustration that much of the literature in this field has set out to offer the world of higher education guidance in, and examples of, the implementation of problem-based learning but little, in real terms, that deals with the difficulties and complexities of the approach. Problem-based learning is something to get excited about, it is an approach that *does* matter, because through its implementation it is possible to provide many rich and innovative opportunities, which will help improve student learning. To begin to see these kinds of possibilities through problem-based learning is to begin to realize its value to the world of higher education and the world of work. Problem-based learning can help students to *learn with complexity*, to see that there are no straightforward answers to problem scenarios, but that learning and life takes place in contexts, contexts which affect the kinds of solutions that are available and possible. Learning such as this is not just a straightforward method of solving problems, but it helps people to learn how to learn and to link learning with their own interests and motivations. It can help students to learn in the context of 'real life' and focus the explorations they undertake, when engaging with problem-based learning, on their practice.

Current problem-based learning literature centres predominantly upon important concerns about ways in which problem-based learning is seen, used and implemented. Texts that offer helpful guidance, that explain curricula change and demonstrate the value of problem-based learning to staff and students are numerous. Whilst these are not only useful but vital to enable others to implement problem-based learning, in the main they tend to portray a positive world in which problem-based learning 'works' and is valued. These texts are important in enabling us to make changes and to move towards curricula that are problem-based, yet at the same time they also portray a world that exists for few. Furthermore, there is a certain expectation that problem-based learning can and will make a difference but often the reality of the expected differences in learners' lives is not articulated. For example, there is little research to date that has explored the impact of problem-based learning upon staff and students' lives or examined the impact of implementing problem-based learning upon the institution, or the impact of implementing problem-based learning in an institution set up for lecture-based learning. Such personal and organizational concerns need to be highlighted and engaged with in ways that do justice to staff, students and institutions involved in problem-based learning. It will then be possible to see that problem-based learning involves more than just curricula innovation and change, and encompasses a greater challenge than just meeting issues and concerns on the UK Government's agenda, such as lifelong learning and skills for life and work.

This book, therefore, sets out to embrace and value the current research and literature in the field of problem-based learning to date, but it also takes a step further. What is offered here is a theoretical framework that emerged from staff and student data. The example of the students at the beginning of the chapter is just one of the 'real life' stories that emanated from these data. In the field of qualitative research the ideal is to allow theories to ensue from data, but despite what is espoused, models and frameworks are imposed all too often on data in ways that do not allow for the emergence of human action and experience. The framework presented here evolved from my own sense making and engagement with the perspectives of those involved in problem-based learning programmes. Inevitably my own experience of problem-based learning as a former facilitator, as a consultant and as a researcher was part of that sense making but the framework was not imposed, instead it emerged from the lives of those involved in the study. This is a conception, a theoretical language in which students' voices are central to the understanding of the framework of Dimensions of Learner Experience.

What I am arguing for are new perspectives, different truths about what is really occurring on problem-based learning curricula and in the lives of those involved with them. The consideration of personal experience in learning is something that is noticeably lacking in the literature about learning in general, and problem-based learning in particular, yet for many, personal experience is that which makes learning both possible and meaningful. New definitions and new meanings of learning often emerge when the interaction of ideas and experiences collide with one another. They also arise through forms of learning, such as problem-based learning, that challenge our very selves. Textbooks in the field seem to relate little to the actual stories being told during my own research and by colleagues implementing problem-based learning: ways in which learners and teachers managed complex and diverse learning in the context of their lives in a fragile and often incoherent world. These are the untold stories.

Learning . . .

The continuing debates about the nature and process of adult learning have created a minefield of overlapping concepts, with few clear frameworks for understanding the relationship between the context and the experience of the learner. Traditionally, learning theories have been grouped into categories, from the behavioural traditions through to the critical awareness theorists, but with full acknowledgment that one may overlap with another.

However, those in the field of critical awareness have argued that theirs is not simply another perspective on adult learning but rather a shift in ideology. The ideals of this tradition stem largely from theorists, such as Freire (1972, 1974), who argued that social and historical forces shape the processes through which people come to know themselves and develop their view of the world. Learning is therefore seen to occur in a social and cultural context and this necessarily influences what and how people learn. Learners, therefore, must seek to transcend the constraints their world places on them in order to liberate themselves and become critically aware.

Yet the promoters of the cognitive tradition (Ausubel *et al.*, 1978) have argued that new information has to be interpreted in terms of both prior knowledge and shared perspectives. Thus, the existing cognitive structure is the principal factor influencing meaningful learning. In practice this means that meaningful material can only be learned in relation to a previously learned background of relevant concepts. One of the central issues to emerge from this tradition was that of the 'learning context', which will be explored further in Chapter 2. The notion of learning context is important because although students' learning strategies and the processes they have adopted do have a certain stability over time, the learning context affects the quality of student learning (Marton *et al.*, 1984). The acknowledgment of the importance of the learning context has thus begun to raise concerns not only about student learning *per se*, but also has brought to the fore the importance of the learner as a person whose experience is often somewhat marginalized in studies about ways in which students learn.

Those in the humanistic field (Rogers, 1969) contend that significant learning is to be obtained only within situations that are both defined by, and under the control of, the learner. Here the aims of education are on self-development and the development of a fully functioning person. The prior experience of the learner is acknowledged and it is also recognized that students may be constrained by their own negative experiences of learning. The teacher (termed, in this tradition, facilitator) helps to provide a supportive environment in which learners are enabled to recognize and explore their needs. Learning in this tradition is seen as involving the whole person, and not just the intellect, thus educators in this tradition aim to liberate learners and allow them freedom to learn (Boud, 1989).

Finally, the developmental theorists offer us models that in many ways seem to take account of cognition and development. The teacher's concern here is in enabling students to develop both understandings of the nature of knowledge and ways of handling different conceptions of the world, so that knowledge acquisition is seen as an active process. It has been from this field that a number of innovative studies have arisen. For example, from a qualitative study of men at Harvard, Perry devised nine positions that described how students' conceptions of the nature and origins of knowledge evolved (Perry, 1970, 1988). This classic study put issues of learner experience centre stage and argued that students proceed through a sequence of developmental stages. In this description of the attainment of intellectual and emotional maturity the student moves from an authoritarian, polarized view of the world, through stages of uncertainty and accepting uncertainty, to finally an understanding of the implications of managing this uncertainty. The student then accepts the need for orientation by a commitment to values and eventually gains a distinct identity through a thoughtful and constantly developing commitment to a set of values. Belenky *et al.* (1986) were stimulated by Perry's work to explore diverse women's perspectives, and they identified five categories of 'ways of knowing' and from this drew conclusions about the way women see truth, knowledge and authority. For example, women began from a position of silence where they saw themselves as mindless and voiceless and subject to the whims of external authority. In later stages women constructed knowledge; this was where the women viewed all knowledge as related to the context in which it occurred, and experienced themselves as creators of knowledge. It is the work of these developmental theorists that seems to offer some of the more tenable models of learning. They are models which, to a degree, acknowledge that what is missing from many curricula is a recognition of the role and relevance of learning from and through experience, which can prompt the shaping and reconstructing of people's lives as learners and teachers.

The argument

The central argument of this book is that the potential and influence of problem-based learning is yet to be realized in the context of higher education. My thesis is that problem-based learning is an important approach to learning, based in the experiential learning tradition, which needs to be more centrally located in higher education curricula than it is currently. My argument centres around seven themes, which will recur throughout the book:

1. Problem-based learning as a concept and approach is often misunderstood. This tends to result in mistaken perceptions about the possibilities for its use in higher education.
2. Problem-based learning has often been confused with forms of problem-solving learning, which has resulted in the terms being used interchangeably. In some cases this has meant that problem-based learning has been interpreted too narrowly and utilized in limited ways.
3. Misunderstandings of problem-based learning have resulted in an underestimation of its value in terms of equipping students for a complex and changing professional life and the opportunities that can be gained through it to improve student learning.
4. There exist a number of *forms* of problem-based learning but decisions about which form to adopt is rarely made explicit by staff in curricula documents or to the students involved in the programmes. These different forms need to be made explicit as each offers different advantages and emphases to the students, the academe and to the world of work.

5. There is, as yet, little known about what actually occurs, as it were, *inside* problem-based curricula in terms of staff's and students' 'lived experience' of the curriculum. This has consequences. First, students', and to some degree staff's, voices are largely missing from the literature on problem-based learning. Second, key elements such as learning context, learner identity and 'learning in relation' are rarely acknowledged or discussed when implementing or enacting problem-based learning.
6. Learning should be seen as a cyclical process in which students make *transitions* through which they develop increasing (and also sometimes decreasing) understandings of themselves, their context, and the ways and situations in which they learn effectively.
7. The full potential of problem-based learning will only be achieved through:

   - understanding and acknowledging the similarities and differences between problem-based learning and problem-solving learning
   - making the form of problem-based learning on offer explicit
   - recognizing the impact of the organization upon the implementation and enactment of problem-based learning
   - acknowledging that problem-based learning can offer staff and students the opportunity of learning to 'make sense' for themselves, personally, pedagogically and interactionally
   - realizing the value and complexity of it as an approach to learning and the ways in which it can help students to understand and challenge their situations and frameworks by encouraging them to *learn with complexity* and through ambiguity.

The plan

Part 1 begins by exploring problem-based learning through an analysis of its theoretical and philosophical underpinnings and examining the reasons for its growing popularity in the context of worldwide change in higher education. Chapters 1 and 2 focus specifically on how the value of problem-based learning in the context of a learning society has been underestimated. Within these chapters it is also argued that there is work to be done in deepening understandings of the nature and guises of problem-based learning. These chapters provide the platform for the development of the argument that discussions about problem-based learning should be firmly located within a language of experiential learning.

Part 2 explores both the theory and the practice of problem-based learning in the context of four British universities. It presents and then examines the framework of learning that emerged from research and that has subsequently been developed in practice. Four short curricular case studies in Chapter 3 demonstrate the multidimensional nature of problem-based learning within different disciplines and educational environments. The focus of Chapter 4 is on a new framework for understanding the nature of learner experience on problem-based learning programmes that arose from a cross-site investigation into problem-based learning. This framework, termed 'Dimensions of Learner Experience', and the concepts of *personal stance, pedagogical stance and interactional stance* are presented and examined from a theoretical and practical perspective. Chapter 5 argues that students are offered, through problem-based learning, opportunities to recognize and value their learning experiences and to develop independence in inquiry. These opportunities can promote transitions in learning. This chapter fleshes out the framework of Dimensions of Learner Experience by using students' data to demonstrate personal, pedagogical and interactional concerns. It also examines some of the ways in which problem-based learning fosters transitions in students' learning from disjunction to integration and vice versa, in preparation for the next section.

Part 3 explores ways of understanding and implementing principal ideas and challenges that emerged from the framework of Dimensions of Learner Experience. It centres on making sense of problem-based learning and managing its implementation and utilization at a number of different levels. The section begins, in Chapter 6, by documenting the ways in which staff, students and course designers may be enabled to recognize, acknowledge and act on the existence of disjunction so that it can be managed effectively at an individual and organizational level. It examines students' experiences of disjunction in the context of a series of catalysts. Chapter 7 explores the nature of transitions and argues that transitions are not something for which students should take total responsibility. This chapter also explores the extent to which problem-based learning programmes offer greater opportunities for effective management of transitions than do more traditional lecture-based programmes. Chapter 8 concludes this section by exploring the rival agenda in higher education and the fragility of learning environments that necessarily impinge upon problem-based programmes.

The final two chapters of the book locate problem-based learning in the world of higher education in general. Chapter 9 begins by exploring, in brief, the ways in which interpretations of knowledge and learning, and conceptions of the learner, affect how problem-based learning is played out in practice. The rest of the chapter presents and explores five models of problem-based learning. Chapter 10 concludes the book by considering the implications of implementing problem-based learning both for management and organizations in general. It explores some of the current political issues that have organizational and educational implications and discusses the ways in which organizational structures can impinge upon problem-based learning.

Part 1

A Web of Belief?

Part 1

1

Problem-based Learning
Underestimated

Introduction

The central argument of this book is that problem-based learning needs
to be located more centrally in the world of higher education than it is
currently. Through this chapter the concept of problem-based learning is
examined in order to explore both competing understandings of problem-
based learning and underlying reasons for its use and increasing popularity.
It is argued that problem-based learning is not just a different method or
style of teaching. Instead it is a different philosophical approach to the whole
notion of teaching and learning. For example, I argue that at the heart of
this approach is the development of important abilities, such as flexibility,
adaptability, problem-solving and critique. Abilities such as these have been
highlighted by government and industry as central to the development of
future professionals. Whilst the current trend in many universities is to
provide programmes for skills development, such as negotiation, group work,
team work and presentation skills, the advantage which problem-based learning offers is the development of such skills in a learning environment where
they are part of a wider learning approach. This chapter demonstrates the
ways in which a critical understanding of problem-based learning can
broaden perspectives about what is actually on offer through this approach.
However, at the same time it is also important to examine and question
some of the agenda that have prompted the implementation of problem-
based learning in the context of worldwide change in higher education.
Thus, the latter section of the chapter explores some of the reasons why
problem-based learning may have been underestimated or, in some cases,
implemented under rather questionable circumstances.

The emergence of problem-based learning

The notion of learning through solving or managing problems is not new, as
the introduction shows. However, the emergence of problem-based learning

as a specific concept and approach emanated from the work of Barrows, who discovered through his research into medical education that 'medical students and residents for the most part did not seem to think at all. Some gathered data ritualistically and then tried to add it up afterwards, while others came up with a diagnosis based on some symptom or sign, never considering possible alternatives' (Barrows and Tamblyn, 1980: xi). Problem-based learning was developed at McMaster University in Canada where Barrows set out to design a medical school curriculum based solely on small group, student-centred learning. The rationale for problem-based learning stemmed from years of observing experts engaged in clinical reasoning, resulting in Barrows and Tamblyn (1980) claiming that problem-based learning was based on two assumptions. The first was that learning through problem situations was much more effective than memory-based learning for creating a usable body of knowledge. The second was that the medical skills that were most important for treating patients were problem-solving skills, rather than memorization. Yet, what was important about the approach adopted at McMaster was that the focus was not on problem-solving learning whereby individual students were expected to answer a series of questions from information supplied by a lecturer. Instead they were asked, in small teams, to explore a problem situation. Through such an exploration students were expected to examine the gaps in their own knowledge and skills in order to decide what information they needed to acquire in order to resolve or manage the situation with which they were presented.

As Barrows and Tamblyn's model was being developed during the early 1970s there was also increasing interest in the medical world in students' ability to develop problem-solving skills. Other research indicated that medical students were lacking in problem-solving skills (see for example McGuire, 1972, 1985). In parallel, there was interest in understanding students' approaches to problem-solving activities and with it came criticism of the unnaturalness of much laboratory research in cognitive psychology (Neisser, 1982). This resulted in wide-ranging studies of students' problem-solving abilities with a growing emphasis on the use of qualitative methods (Laurillard, 1979, 1984). This early research into problem-solving and clinical decision making prompted interest and research within professions allied to medicine (for example Higgs, 1990; Terry and Higgs, 1993). There was, however, a shift away from focusing on the generation and testing of hypotheses as a means of arriving at a major clinical decision, and a greater emphasis on clinical reasoning as a process occurring throughout clinical practice. This work in part stemmed from some of the early studies into problem-based learning where it was increasingly seen that learning problem-solving abilities in situations isolated from a relevant context did not facilitate effective transference to the clinical environment. What became increasingly apparent was that although problem-solving skills were a useful acquisition for students, it was the application of such skills to a clinical situation that was vital. This was because problem-solving learning tended in the main to be seen as a step by step approach to solving a problem that denied the complexities and difficulties of a clinical situation. In contrast, problem-based learning confronts students with the challenge to manage a clinical situation, which requires them to incorporate diverse resources such as existing knowledge, data collection, interpersonal skills, reflection and reasoning ability in order to meet that challenge.

The bulk of the literature in the late 1970s and 1980s argued for the use of problem-based learning (including, and beyond, the original reasons suggested by Barrows and Tamblyn 1980) for four key reasons. These were, first, to develop students' reasoning skills; second, to enable learning to take place within a context that was relevant to the students; third, to ensure that learning was attuned to the world of work; and finally to promote students' self-directed learning abilities, that is, learning that fostered independent enquiry. A number of articles at that time cited lists of advantages of problem-based learning over more traditional ways of learning (Neame, 1982; Coles, 1985) and others suggested that problem-based learning was found to be more enjoyable and stimulating by staff and students involved in such programmes (Olson, 1987). However, few seemed to tackle many of the underlying assumptions of problem-based learning or relate such assumptions to current trends in the broader context of changes within higher and professional education.

There has been a shift in recent years away from literature that describes problem-based learning, and how it is working in particular courses, towards critical analyses of problem-based learning, which are more sensitive to the complexities of this approach to learning and teaching. This demonstrates the increasing move away from the 1980s decade of evangelism (Boud and Feletti, 1997) towards a deeper consideration of the emerging themes and issues. This can be seen in particular through literature that has argued for problem-based learning as being an approach which can be responsive to the needs of the age. In practice, this can be seen in the increasing demand for the development of particular 'skills' within curricula and with it the realization that problem-based learning is a means of helping students developing such skills. Such skills are commonly termed 'key skills' and are the kinds of skills such as working with others, problem-solving and improving personal learning and performance. Key skills are being offered to undergraduates in order to both enhance their degrees and to produce graduates with well-developed personal and interpersonal skills. The development of key skills has become increasingly important as higher education in the 1990s is being encouraged to produce graduates who are flexible and have market-related skills and abilities. At the same time there is a growing awareness that a focus on skills development at the expense of the development of abilities to research and critique information may result in a 'performative slide' (Barnett, 1998). The concept of a performative slide is that in the desire to equip students for life and work there tends to be an increasing focus on what students are able to *do*. Higher education is sliding towards encouraging students to perform rather than to necessarily think and do.

The result is that students are equipped to undertake tasks, to carry out instructions, and to work with others, but they are not necessarily able to analyse or critique the situation in which they find themselves or the information with which they have been presented. Yet what is on offer through problem-based learning are opportunities for students to develop the required key skills but in a context where they are also encouraged to develop the ability to critique issues and information, and to take up a position towards the situation with which they have been presented.

Understandings and interpretations of problem-based learning

In many ways it could be argued that problem-based learning worldwide is in crisis. There is often a feeling, in any field, that things were better in the days when it was clear what was meant and it was understood how things should be. It seemed that there was a time when many believed that everyone either knew or did not know what counted as problem-based learning and what did not. Yet it seems there is a sea change. Most of those who feel that problem-based learning possesses given characteristics and ways of being have adopted outright the model of problem-based learning as laid out by Barrows and Tamblyn (1980). This is the position taken by those who argue for a prescriptive means of implementing problem-based learning and who suggest that unless it is enacted in a specific way then the ability to promote particular learning principles through it is considerably diminished (for example Engel, 1997). However the notion that problem-based learning can be described as something definable that can be contained within boundaries only serves to create two further problems. The first is that these narrow ideals unnecessarily tend to set traditional notions of learning against progressive ones. The second is that it sets up misconceptions about what might be seen and accepted as problem-based learning and what might not. Instead I would argue that problem-based learning has many guises and differences, and that these can stem from the discipline or professional knowledge base into which it is introduced, and/or the structural and pedagogical decisions that have been made during implementation and subsequent enactment. For example, the pedagogical decisions, that is those decisions which relate to the kind of teaching and learning methods that underpin and are adopted in a curriculum, can affect the ways in which problem-based learning is played out in practice. For instance, engineering is a subject that for many years has used problem-solving approaches to learning, largely in the context of lecture-based programmes. The implementation of problem-based learning in engineering may be affected by an overarching pedagogical view, such as the perspective that students require a sound body of knowledge and sufficient mathematical skills before they are knowledgeable enough and equipped to engage with problem-based learning. The result is that problem-based learning is more likely to take place in the third year of such a programme. Other disciplines may be affected by the traditional ways in which they have always been taught and the values and distinctive views of knowledge held by those within them. Contrastingly, there are other subjects, such as those within health sciences, which are based on other subjects and disciplines and are therefore less bounded by a distinct pedagogy of their own. Perhaps it is this lack of a strong underlying disciplinary base that has made it easier for these areas, such as health sciences, to adopt problem-based learning than those subjects with a stronger disciplinary base. Yet at the same time particular traditions and practices can also be an impediment, such as the kinds of traditional views of what was expected of a nurse or a physiotherapist undertaking apprentice-style training where they were required to learn by example and following instructions to the letter.

At this point it is perhaps important to sound a cautionary note. It may seem that I am arguing that all learning is problem-based or that all learning that involves some kind of problem-solving is problem-based learning. The difficulties and dilemmas involved are more complex than this and are related to conceptions of teaching and learning, understandings about what counts as knowledge, and a whole host of other concerns that will be dealt with later in this book. This leaves us with the problem about what it might mean to implement problem-based learning when it is difficult to know what it is that is being attempted. A way forward from this is to argue instead for a set of key characteristics that, within a given context, may come together as a whole to form a problem-based approach. Problem-based learning might then be seen as an ideology rooted in the experiential learning tradition that can be adopted within modules, across semesters or throughout curricula. Boud (1985) and Barrows (1986) both have listed characteristics of problem-based learning. Both have argued that problem-based learning is not to be seen as a particular way or method of learning, rather it is to be seen as learning that has a number of differing forms. Boud (1985) suggested that problem-based learning differs according to the nature of the field and the particular goals of the programme. He noted that developments in problem-based learning have drawn on a number of ideas in addition to problem-centredness, the most important of which he sees as student-centredness. Boud subsequently outlined eight other characteristics of many problem-based learning courses:

1. An acknowledgement of the base of experience of learners.
2. An emphasis on students taking responsibility for their own learning.
3. A crossing of boundaries between disciplines.
4. An intertwining of theory and practice.
5. A focus on the processes of knowledge acquisition rather than the products of such processes.
6. A change in staff role from that of instructor to that of facilitator.
7. A change in focus from staff assessment of outcomes of learning to student self- and peer assessment.

8. A focus on communication and interpersonal skills so that students understand that in order to relate their knowledge, they require skills to communicate with others, skills which go beyond their area of technical expertise.

Barrows has suggested that the combination of design variables for problem-based learning, when linked to the educational objectives, is endless. He concluded that the term problem-based learning must be considered a genus from which there are many species and subspecies. As such, all types of problem-based learning must be evaluated in terms of issues such as the type of scenarios, assessment methods, learners' autonomy and the way in which teaching and learning occurs. Barrows (1986) thus proposed a taxonomy of problem-based learning methods that explains differing meanings and uses of problem-based learning. The taxonomy has highlighted the educational objectives that it is possible to address through problem-based learning and it has included the following combination of varieties in use:

1. Lecture-based cases – here students are presented with information through lectures and then case material is used to demonstrate that information.
2. Case-based lectures – in this instance students are presented with case histories or vignettes before a lecture that then covers relevant material.
3. Case method – students are given a complete case study that must be researched and prepared for discussion in the next class.
4. Modified case-based – here students are presented with some information and are asked to decide on the forms of action and decisions they may make. Following their conclusions, they are provided with more information about the case.
5. Problem-based – in this instance students meet with a client in some form of simulated format that allows for free enquiry to take place.
6. Closed-loop problem-based – this is an extension of the problem-based method, where students are asked to consider the resources they used in the process of problem-solving in order to evaluate how they may have reasoned through the problem more effectively.

The perspectives offered by Barrows and Boud have demonstrated the multifaceted nature of problem-based learning, a position which has been supported and subsequently developed by Margetson in a number of articles during the early 1990s. Margetson (1991b) suggested that problem-based learning should be seen as more than just a different method of learning, but rather as a specific stance towards both knowledge and the position of the student in the learning process. He has argued for a different view of learning and an alternative starting point from traditional approaches to teaching. Problem-based learning may be seen as 'a conception of knowledge, understanding, and education profoundly different from the more usual conception underlying subject-based learning' (Margetson, 1991b: 43–4). Over the past decade, Margetson has tackled a number of the complex issues relating to problem-based learning from a broad philosophical perspective. He has offered some important perspectives to those wishing to understand the philosophical underpinnings of problem-based learning and some of the multifaceted difficulties that emerge when attempting to implement problem-based learning organizationally. Margetson argued in the early 1990s for an examination of the relationship between teaching and facilitation and an exploration of the significance of problem-based learning in relation to current educational reform. Furthermore, he suggested (Margetson, 1991a) that the assumption that 'knowledge is certain' persists and that the assumed link between certainty and knowledge is used to justify lecture-based methods of teaching. Margetson's thought-provoking arguments have been a challenge to many implementing problem-based learning, particularly in the areas of science and medicine where there is often a greater emphasis on acquiring certain knowledge than in the subjects of arts and social science.

Arguments such as this demonstrate that there are not narrowly defined characteristics of problem-based learning. Instead there are people working in contexts using problem-based approaches. Problem-based learning is an approach to learning that is affected by the structural and pedagogical environment into which it is placed, in terms of the discipline or subject, the organization and the staff concerned. As will be seen later, it is possible to articulate overarching features of curricula that use problem-based learning, from which it is possible to formulate broad models. However, since the emergence and popularization of problem-based learning, many have sought to define it in some way. It would seem at first glance that it is only by unpacking characteristics that any comparison about what makes problem-based learning different from other ways of learning is possible. Yet merely to list specific and narrowly defined characteristics does not in fact untangle the philosophical conundrums of problem-based learning. Walton and Matthews (1989) have argued that problem-based learning is to be understood as a general educational strategy rather than merely a teaching approach, and have noted that there was no fixed agreement as to what does and does not constitute problem-based learning. However, they have argued that for problem-based learning to be present, three components must be able to be differentiated. The suggestion that these authors make offers real clarity about how problem-based learning might be seen and understood. They present parameters within which to understand problem-based learning without losing the sense of its vitality and complexity as an approach. The three broad areas of differentiation are as follows:

1. Essential characteristics of problem-based learning that comprised curricula organization around problems rather than disciplines, an integrated curriculum and an emphasis on cognitive skills.
2. Conditions that facilitated problem-based learning such as small groups, tutorial instruction and active learning.

3. Outcomes that were facilitated by problem-based learning such as the development of skills and motivation, together with the development of the ability to be lifelong learners.

This particular interpretation of problem-based learning offers modes of understanding this educational strategy that take account of the complex nature of learning. At the same time it is an interpretation that encapsulates the differing ways in which students learn in diverse professions across a variety of institutions.

Problem-based learning in the changing terrain of higher education

Over the past few decades there has been increasing pressure on higher education worldwide to re-examine and make explicit its aims and outcomes. In the United Kingdom (UK) the move towards a market model of higher education, that is a model of higher education which is responsive to market demands and forces in the wider society, has paralleled increasing demand for accountability to the public and State and for greater vocational relevance. This shift towards, and openness to, market forces has resulted in closer links between higher education and industry. This has promoted changes in curricula generally, in particular the development of personal qualities for life and work exemplified through the growth of key skills programmes in higher education curricula. Expansion in higher education, with the move towards a mass rather than an élite system has to some extent occurred through the widening of access and the continuing attempts to broaden the social mix in higher education. Innovations such as National Vocational Qualifications (NVQ), access courses and the accreditation of prior experiential learning (APEL) have meant that the clientele within the system has changed, albeit slowly, bringing new challenges and complexities. For example, a more diverse student population than former years requires a broader range of teaching and learning methods, which can take account of a variety of student learning needs and study patterns. Flexible approaches to learning and new and different forms of distance education are just a few of the recent demands diverse students require of the higher education system. Such demands have caused many departments to consider such approaches as problem-based learning to take account of students' requirements (for example Taylor and Burgess, 1995).

New debates about professional education have also been influential in putting problem-based learning high on the agenda within higher education. For example, Eraut (1985) argued that higher education needed to develop a role beyond that of creating and transmitting knowledge, by enhancing the knowledge creation capacity of individual and professional communities. This would therefore require a greater exchange between higher education and professions. Arguments such as this have prompted discussions around the nature of knowledge and the ways in which knowledge is used and perceived in the context of professional education. Others have explored the nature of different types of professional curricula and suggested that the integration of theory and practice within professional curricula was vital, and that this integration should be seen in terms of the worth of, and consequent assessment of, practice within the curriculum. Such research and literature have prompted the incorporation of ways of helping students to understand how practitioners think and reflect in action into both curricula and professional practice. One such way was seen to be the inclusion of problem-based learning within professional curricula (for example Sadlo, 1994; Cawley, 1997) and more recently the shifts towards valuing and accrediting initiatives such as work-based learning.

Professional education is an area that has grown and developed through a number of changes since the 1960s and Barnett (1990) has argued that the growth of professional education is possibly the most significant feature of development of higher education in the UK over the past 30 years. The largest area of growth in the use of problem-based learning is in the area of professional education. This can be seen in the diversity of literature and texts that offer guidance to those in professional education wanting to implement problem-based learning (for example Alavi, 1995; Boud and Feletti, 1997; Taylor, 1997; Glen and Wilkie, 1999). Problem-based learning is also increasingly being seen in professional education as a means of managing the growing and widening knowledge base of individual professions, since curricula can no longer expand to cope with such demands. As a result students in professional education are increasingly being equipped to 'manage knowledge' rather than being expected to have assimilated it all before qualification. Thus it can be seen that experimentation around the use of problem-based learning has been shaped by new questions being raised about professional education in the context of unprecedented world expansion in higher education during the 1960s and again during the 1980s and late 1990s. Change in the UK appeared to have emerged as a result of the government's growing demand for greater accountability within education and employers' preferences for graduate entrants with key skills. This is seen, too, in such examples as the report *Tomorrow's Doctors* (General Medical Council, 1993), which recognized the merits of learner-centred and problem-orientated approaches to learning, and strongly encouraged the adoption of these approaches within British medical schools. Following their entry into higher education, a number of nursing schools in the UK also committed varying proportions of their new curricula to problem-based learning.

Despite the value seen by many in the implementation of problem-based learning, there is also a need to be careful that it is taken up for sound reasons and it is not adopted in ways that go down the slippery slope towards the performative slide. To focus too much on what students are able to do and on their ability to perform, could be to deny many students the vital opportunities to critique the situations and information with which they are being presented. Yet the adoption of problem-based learning sometimes occurs on the one hand because it is seen as an innovative means of managing curricula difficulties or introducing innovation in teaching and learning (Silver *et al.*, 1997). On the other hand it may have been implemented because it is seen to offer opportunities to call for the end of knowledge, disciplines and staff–student boundaries, an end befitting a fragmented, ambiguous postmodernity. There appears to be a number of inter-related reasons for the increasing popularity of problem-based learning while at the same time there is an apparent underestimation of it as a catalyst for change within curricula and a prompt to transitions in people's lives. Yet problem-based learning has been underestimated in a variety of ways which means that it is not yet located centrally within the higher education system.

Problem-based learning underestimated?

Although problem-based learning has so far been underestimated in terms of its overall use value in higher education, there are clear signs of its growth and increasingly popularity. This is important, but what is of concern is that it is not always supported in the growth areas by the organization into which it is placed, and thus although there is growth, to some extent much of this is at the marginalized end of the system (see for example the findings of the study into innovation undertaken by Silver *et al.*, 1997). However, the popularity of problem-based learning does also seem to be occurring due to a series of trends, some of which could be said to have dubious motives behind them. These can be mapped as follows.

Labour market demands for key skills

Problem-based learning offers opportunities for students to learn in teams, develop presentation skills, learn negotiation abilities and develop research skills and many other abilities. Such skills and abilities are highly valued by a variety of public and private sector clients, who are playing an increasing role in UK higher education. Problem-based learning is clearly recognized as offering students a means of acquiring such skills and abilities in the context of curricula where it then becomes unnecessary to bolt on extra sessions to enable students to acquire market related skills. The value here is in the centralization of activities in problem-based learning curricula, which can prompt students to engage not only with skills for life and work, but also to develop an ability to critique, instead of fragmenting the nurturing of particular activities through skills training sessions. The disadvantage is that problem-based learning can be seen as the sole means of 'giving students skills' rather than implementing problem-based learning with a clear understanding of the wider pedagogical and organizational implications of its use.

The incorporation into curricula of professional agenda

Interprofessional education is growing in the UK and problem-based learning is increasingly being viewed as a vehicle to promote and implement it. There has been a shift away from forms of shared learning where students of different professional groups, as it were, 'share' the same learning experience by receiving lectures and seminars on subjects of common ground. Instead there is an increasing desire for forms of learning to occur in which students engage with each other through debate, group work and problem-based learning, in which they are educated with and through each other. Such forms of learning, defined here as interprofessional education, seek to enable students to develop sound understandings of different professional perspectives, to understand the similarities and differences between them, and to encourage an exploration of discipline and subject boundaries. Students are also helped to experience the different ways in which professions utilize the same knowledge in different ways.

The desire to marry problem-based learning with interprofessional education has emerged through a realization that, brought together, these educational approaches can help students to engage with and manage many of the barriers and difficulties of working in interprofessional teams. The introduction of either shared learning or interprofessional education ideas into the undergraduate curriculum can seek to meet this need for interdisciplinary understanding at an early stage of the young professional's working life. Shared learning is seen as any learning or teaching in which participants are drawn from two or more professional groups (Barr, 1994), and may include workshops and seminars as well as lectures. Interprofessional education uses a variety of teaching methods and learning strategies to encourage interaction and interactive learning across the professions. The aims of interprofessional education are likely to include the development of skills and attitudes as well as knowledge, whereas shared learning may have more limited aims.

Integrating these two approaches can help students to not only learn about team work but also what it means to work in an effective team. Thus in the UK, agencies such as the National Health Service (NHS) National Training Forum and the NHS Training Authority have supported interprofessional education. Health service consortia are promoting problem-based learning in the context of interprofessional education in order to develop professionals of the future who are flexible and adaptable, but also because there appears to be a belief that interprofessional education is cost effective and thus economically worthwhile. Over time it might be that the financial pressures on the NHS and higher education will mean that there is increasing support for a method such as problem-based learning, which is expected to meet multiple aims and decreased funding requirements.

The declining unit of resource in higher education

There has been a fall of over 30 per cent in the public funding that UK universities have received per student since 1980 (Williams and Fry, 1994), and the cuts continue. In the shift from an élite to a mass system there has been an increased participation in higher education compared with former years, with the result that university resources are increasingly overstretched. Large student numbers, decreasing resources and overextended staff is beginning to characterize the state of higher education worldwide. For some, problem-based learning is seen as a means of teaching a larger group of more diverse students than in former years, using less face to face contact. For example, if students are learning in groups without a member of staff to facilitate the process, then staff can be available to undertake research and other activities that may help the survival of their department. A more cynical perspective is to suggest that new and more interesting ways of learning than lecture-based learning, such as problem-based learning are likely to attract students because they provide 'infotainment'; a liberal mix of information and entertainment (Ritzer, 1996). Ritzer has suggested that:

> In addition to the demands of increasingly consumerist parents and students, the pressure on colleges and universities to change is being fueled by economic factors, especially the relative decline in funding of higher education. With outside funding being reduced, the university responds, among other ways, by cutting costs and by attempting to attract and keep more new (and paying) 'customers'. The new means of consumption are attractive models because they not only excel at attracting customers, but also at reducing costs.
>
> (Ritzer, 1996: 188)

This kind of infotainment will be particularly evident in curricula that include the added attraction of information technology and distance learning components. Students will see kinds of learning such as this as efficient, independent, low cost and fun. Thus, universities who utilize problem-based learning 'infotainment-style' will expect to attract more students whilst at the same time reducing costs.

'It seemed like a good idea'

Problem-based learning is being adopted because it is seen to be fashionable and offers kudos to those involved in curricula innovation and change. For some it may be implemented in order to enhance promotion prospects, for others it is seen as a helpful means of engaging students in learning instead of boredom, while also offering staff themselves a new and entertaining way of teaching for themselves. At an organizational level problem-based learning may be adopted to solve practical curricula difficulties such as merging departments of the same discipline when two institutions unite. Alternatively, problem-based learning may be utilized when large subject areas, such as health sciences, move into the university sector. This has occurred in the UK when two or three Schools of Nursing and Midwifery have amalgamated and are subsequently incorporated into a university. Such schools have invariably been regional satellites with different curricula and pedagogical emphases. In instances such as this, problem-based learning has been adopted as means of managing diverse curricula agenda.

The opportunity to create a 'multi-inclusion' curriculum

Multi-inclusion curricula are, I suggest, the kind of curricula that are designed to enable students to cover a large body of knowledge and develop key skills, whilst providing them with large-scale infotainment by offering a wide variety of opportunities for learning. These kinds of curricula are designed to meet the requirements of multiple stakeholders; students, government, professional bodies, health service consortia and employers. The diversity of learning methods in higher education, along with the knowledge explosion, has meant that many curricula are overcrowded with both content and process. For example in some areas, such as health sciences, problem-based learning has been adopted in recent years for well-thought through pedagogical concerns, of which one has been the difficulty of managing the sheer volume of knowledge and abilities expected by employers in the health and social services. However, at the same time problem-based learning has also been seen as a place where it is possible to add in other interesting methods of learning, some of which are applicable and others which are not. Yet even those which are applicable, such as problem-solving learning packages that contextualize knowledge and provide relevant and meaningful learning experiences, can be overwhelming to the student in the face of so much other change. What can be seen then are curricula that are only problem-based in the sense that the students are so overwhelmed by knowledge(s), modules, distance learning, global study, clinical skills laboratories and web-based assessment that they spend the entire course trying to understand the similarities, differences and interfaces between all the approaches. There is a sense that 'multi-inclusion' curricula can offer too much choice so that ultimately incoherence and diversity created for the students through them can become disabling rather than enabling.

The means of responding to 'directed innovation'

The notion of directed innovation (Silver, 1998) stems from the idea that most innovation that is rewarded is directed by governments and institutions, and is necessarily funded by stakeholders. Therefore, what will be seen here is not guided and self-motivated innovation as in former years, but innovation that is bounded by government policy, funding frameworks and institutional research policies. Problem-based learning is an approach that can also emerge as something which is part of a directed innovation, perhaps to secure monies or grants rather than because of clear pedagogical motivations. For example, industry funding for projects that link together learning technology and problem-based learning reflects the way in which learning can be hijacked to further the cause of university status and the carving out of personal careers supported by government agenda. A sound educational edge could be lost amidst other more tempting sweeteners. That is not to say that we should not take the money and run – but we need to be clear about who wins and loses when we do.

Conclusion

It is important to note that, although problem-based learning would seem to offer multiple advantages to staff, students and employers, the value of this approach from an educational viewpoint has been seriously underestimated. For example, problem-based learning can offer students opportunities to learn how to learn, and to develop key skills, independence in enquiry and the ability to contest and debate. For staff it can offer a means of responding to the problem of ever increasing pressures on curriculum content, opportunities for interprofessional education, and for implementing teaching that is grounded in the world of work, which can stimulate students to engage with the complexity and diversity of everyday problem situations. Problem-based learning can provide a means of managing the kinds of diversity that, amongst other things, offers a range of choice for the educator and the learner. Some of these choices and opportunities may be evident to those currently utilizing problem-based learning but they are rarely made explicit in the literature.

In this first chapter some of the current views, models and assumptions about how problem-based learning is understood have been explored in an attempt to begin to unravel the argument that problem-based learning has been underestimated, undervalued and misunderstood in the world of higher education. The lack of studies into what actually occurs inside problem-based curricula adds fuel to this argument because as a result there is, as yet, little known about staff's and students' 'lived experience' of the curriculum. The consequence of this is that because students', and to some degree staff's, voices are largely missing from the literature on problem-based learning, key elements such as learning context, learner identity and 'learning in relation' are rarely acknowledged or discussed when implementing or enacting problem-based learning. The next chapter examines these three elements that tend to be increasingly omitted from discussions concerning the implementation and enactment of problem-based learning in today's climate.

2

Missing Elements

A group of eight first year nursing students sit chatting around a table whilst examining the contents of a large box. The box contains a number of cartoons, photographs and newspaper cuttings of nurses. There is a sheet of paper on which two questions are posed. Someone reads them out: 'What images are commonly held in society about nurses. In what ways might these perceptions affect the relationship between how you see yourself as a nurse and how others see you?' There is silence. Students rifle through papers and fiddle with pens. As they move to explore the images a discussion begins. There seems to be a confusion amongst the students about the way nurses are seen differently in different contexts. This prompts a heated debate about what it means to be a nurse personally and professionally. As the students leave the room an hour or so later one of them reflects with surprise, 'I learnt a lot from other people's experiences but I didn't realize that other students' perspectives and my own previous experiences were relevant to this course until now.'

This scenario will be familiar to some of those who have used small group work in higher education or industry. It will perhaps be more familiar to those who have been using problem-based learning. So what is the significance of this scenario? It demonstrates that there are ways in which problem-based learning can help students to own their own learning experiences, and to value and learn from peers' perspectives in ways that help them to make sense of their own frameworks and situations. Problem-based learning can help students to realize, often early on in a programme, that professional life demands the management of difficult and often competing agenda. Learning about, and through, these kinds of challenges brings to the fore three important elements that are made explicit through this type of approach. This is because problem-based learning raises students' awareness about their perspectives and values in a context that is centred in the world of work for which they are being educated. It is also because, through learning in a team, students are prompted to work and learn collaboratively in ways that mirror professional life. The three elements that are central to problem-based learning are: learner identity, learning context, and 'learning in relation'. However, before these elements are explored and a case made for their particular importance, it is necessary to consider what it means to be a learner in higher education.

Being a learner

Many lecturers and mentors will have considered what it is like to be a learner in higher education. Some will not. Yet assumptions about what it means to be a learner affect the approaches staff take towards students both personally and pedagogically, that is in terms of the teaching and learning approaches which they value and implement. It is often suggested that the ways in which staff have been taught are reflected in the ways in which they subsequently teach their own students. However, changes in the role, diversity and number of students have resulted in shifting perceptions about what it means to learn and to be a learner in higher education. There are lecturers who complain that students are 'not as bright as they used to be' and others who are astounded that students can revise for examinations listening to rock music and television and still achieve a first class degree. Yet there is a growing realization that there is in fact little real understanding about how students see themselves and what learning means to them. For example, pilot projects, which have examined schoolchildren's cognitive ability to process multiple information inputs simultaneously, suggest that higher education for the learner of the future will need to look very different in order to maintain interest for learners (Heppell, 1995). Heppell's study analysed schoolchildren's ability to watch three or four different television programmes simultaneously. What was found to be significant was not that the children coped with watching all the programmes but that the strategies they used to do this were effective, complex and sophisticated. Heppell suggested that these children were 'internalising their personal interpretation of a media text from multiple media sources which they structure and decode through a complex familiarity with the grammar and syntax of the media they enjoy in their everyday lives' (Heppell, 1995: 4). Projects such as these challenge the values that underpin such activities as the single medium lecture, and suggest that learners of the future will use multiple and possibly very different strategies for learning from those with which they are currently presented in higher education.

Just as there is little understanding about what goes on inside curricula in general, in terms of the role and relevance of learning from experience (Boud *et al.*, 1993), there is still relatively little insight into the ways in which students engaged in problem-based learning use experience for learning. For example, what does it mean to 'know' in a problem-based learning context? How do students understand the difference in relationship between being a student in a lecture and being a student in a problem-based seminar? Some of the difficulties experienced in the 'lived' curriculum for students emerge from conflicts about managing work schedules and standards, researching information, understanding what counts as a thorough presentation, all in the context of being an individual within a problem-based learning team. There are a number of authors who have discussed the importance of learner experience in such a context. For example, Ryan (1993) sought to identify whether students felt that it was important to be self-directed as learners. He also explored whether these student perceptions changed as they moved through the course, and suggested that problem-based learning incorporated the development of 'self-directed learning ability' and that the development of this ability was essential to problem-based learning. His study showed that students perceived self-directed learning to be important, and that the importance increased significantly throughout the semester, but felt this might be due to the highly supportive learning environment. However, Ryan did not really address the issue of whether, because of students' differing perceptions of self-directed learning, they were either better or worse at problem-based learning or found it more or less useful for themselves as learners.

Dolmans and Schmidt (1994) studied the extent to which various elements of problem-based learning curricula influenced students' self-study patterns. They found that the availability of a reference list, course objectives, lectures, the tutor and the existence of tests and examinations all had an impact on the students' learning activities during self-study. First year students were found to rely more on reference lists and content covered in lectures, while students in later years were shown to be more self-directed and relied less on lectures and reference lists. Yet their study did not address the way in which this increase in self-direction occurred, nor did it explore the reasons why first year students adopted different approaches. Perhaps what materialized in this course actually applies to many curricula, whether problem-based or traditional, since first year students tend to be cue-seekers who actively look for assistance from staff to help them play the assessment game (Miller and Parlett, 1974) but later often become self-directed as their programme progresses. However, a more recent study (Taylor and Burgess, 1995) documented the findings of an illuminative evaluation of a problem-based learning course in social work. The study showed that students starting the course were at different stages of readiness for self-directed learning. Students, with the benefit of hindsight, felt that four areas could usefully have been included within an orientation programme to have facilitated their introduction to problem-based learning. These were the lecturers' expectations of self-directed learning, the role of the facilitator, the principles and practices of learning in groups, and issues of time management. In response to these findings a lecture was introduced to present the philosophy and structure of problem-based learning and a series of voluntary exercises were made available for group use. These included exercises on chairing a meeting and giving and receiving feedback. Research findings indicated that all groups chose to undergo at least one of the exercises. Taylor and Burgess concluded that more attention could be paid in course design to the process of preparing students for self-directed learning.

It seems that although many who have adopted problem-based learning espouse the importance of learner autonomy, self-direction and group work and argue for students developing 'constructed knowledge' (Belenky *et al.*, 1986), there is actually little research that has explored these areas. The notion of constructed knowledge is based on the assumption that knowledge is related to the context in which it occurs and is applied, and that students see themselves as creators of knowledge. Yet in many undergraduate and preregistration curricula, even those that utilize problem-based learning, there still appears to be an emphasis on knowledge acquisition rather than knowledge creation. Thus, students are expected to collect the body of knowledge relevant to their subject rather than encouraged to explore and create knowledge for themselves. Within the small body of research into students' experiences of problem-based learning there is little documentation of students' understanding of what it means to be autonomous or self-directed, or the kinds of changes they experience when learning through problem-based learning compared with traditional teaching methods. Yet different notions and interpretations of self-direction by staff and students may produce learning experiences for students characterized by confusion and conflict. For example, some students may choose to learn in isolation and adopt an individualistic approach to studying, which can result in the kinds of surface approaches to learning characterized by students being merely efficient data processors instead of being participants in a dialogic process (Wildemeersch, 1989; Savin-Baden, 1996). The concept of surface approaches to learning emerged from the work of Marton and Säljö (1984) who distinguished two different approaches to learning: those learners who could concentrate on memorizing what the author wrote (surface level learning) and those who gave the authors' words meaning in their own terms (deep level learning). Surface level learning is characterized by a reproductive concept of learning, which means that the learner is more or less forced to adopt a rote learning strategy. Deep level learning is characterized by 'making sense'; comprehension of what is being said by an author in the text. However, students may also become isolated through self-directed learning because of the expectation by peers, tutor or both that self-direction is necessarily empowering when in practice it is not.

Tennant has argued that assumptions about adult learning, and those held by Knowles (1978) in particular, are shrouded by myths such as 'the myth that our need for self-direction is rooted in our constitutional make-up; the myth that self-development is a process of change, towards higher levels of existence; and the myth that adult learning is fundamentally (and necessarily) different from child learning' (Tennant, 1986: 121). Arguments such as this raise questions as to the ideological claims about notions of self-directed learning and autonomy, and understandings about what might constitute learning that takes place in a relevant context. Although it is possible to map some of these dilemmas, there are issues about context and identity that are also central to this argument.

Recognizing the missing elements

This section outlines the concepts of learner identity, learning context and 'learning in relation'. Recognizing and valuing these elements, in the sense of understanding the essential qualities and boundaries of these concepts, is vital to a kind of higher education that equips students to learn with complexity, that is an ability to engage with coherence and incoherence, consensus and dissensus as well as the vicissitudes of an uncertain and globalized world. It is through engaging with the complex interaction of self, context and others that students are challenged and enabled to critique their own frameworks as well as those of others, so that they are equipped to engage with and manage different and sometimes conflicting perspectives. Thus it will become evident that these elements are important not only to problem-based learning but also to the future of learning in higher education in general.

Learner identity

Learner identity (after Weil, 1986) is used here to express the idea that the interaction of learner and learning, in whatever framework, formulates a particular kind of identity. The notion of learner identity moves beyond, but encapsulates the notion of learning style, and encompasses positions that students take up in learning situations, whether consciously or unconsciously. There needs to be a recognition that learners must be defined by more than just their learning styles. The concept of learning styles has suggested that an individual has a consistent approach to organizing information and processing it in the learning environment, yet the model of learning styles developed by Kolb and Fry (1975), in which they suggest there are four learning styles: converger, diverger, assimilator and accommodator, is rather too tidy. They argue that a complete learner is someone who has managed to integrate bipolar components of the four learning styles. Although this is a useful model for helping learners to understand something of their approach to learning, it is problematic in that different learning environments demand different learning styles and thus the complete learner must be someone who can either adapt their style or someone who applies a consistent learning strategy across all environments. Furthermore, invariably school leavers have an identity largely formulated through their schooling, and they arrive at university with a sense of whether they are deemed to be successes or failures by peers and external authorities. These students understand themselves in terms of how they are seen as learners by others. They realize components of their learner identity through the eyes of others, even if they cannot define it for themselves. For other students learner identity is not related to how they are seen by others but instead through the conditions under which they perceive themselves to be learning. This reflects the conditions in which learning, for them, takes place. Thus, learner identity incorporates not just a sense of how one has come to be a learner in a given context, but also the perceptions about when and how one actually learns. As a result, this identity also encompasses affective components of learning that often seem of little matter to those in the business of creating learning environments in institutional settings. Issues of trust and fear that emerge through critical reflection such as questioning, reframing assumptions, learning together, sharing and evaluating researched information, undertaking presentations and arguing one's point are rarely acknowledged in learning environments (Brookfield, 1994). Still, learner identity is not to be seen as a stable entity but as something people use to make sense of themselves, and the ways in which they learn best in relation to other people and the learning environments in which they are learning.

Bernstein (1992) has argued that through their experiences as students, individuals within higher education are in the process of identity formation. He has suggested that this process may be seen as the construction of pedagogic identities, which will change according to the different relationships that occur between society, higher education and knowledge. Pedagogic identities are defined as those that 'arise out of contemporary culture and technological change that emerge from dislocations, moral, cultural, economic and are perceived as the means of regulating and effecting change' (Bernstein, 1992: 3). Thus, pedagogic identities are characterized by the emphases of the time. For example, in the traditional disciplines of the 1960s, students were inducted into the particular pedagogical customs of those disciplines, whereas pedagogic identities of the 1990s were characterized by a common set of market-related, transferable skills. The difference between the two identities is that, while pedagogic identities are seen to be those that arise out of contemporary culture and technological change, learner identities emerge from the process through which students seek to transcend subjects, disciplines and the structures embedded in higher education. Thus, in developing learner identities, some students are enabled to shift beyond frameworks that are imposed by culture, validated through political agenda or supplied by academics. They are facilitated in developing for themselves, possibly through an approach such as problem-based learning, the formulation of a learner identity that emerges from challenging the frameworks, rather than having those systems and frameworks imposed upon them.

There is a threat, however, to learner identity. The shift to performative agendas, characterized by the performative slide, in higher education along with the kind of technology that only promotes individualized, solitary, virtual learning environments can mean that students are denied opportunities to formulate their learner identities. Students' ability to make sense for themselves is at risk in a performative society because of the way in which the culture of such a society necessarily means that knowledge and skills are defined for the student by society, and as interpreted by academic staff, in the quest to operationalize learning. It has been argued that:

The technology is changing rapidly but underlying constructivist models of learning are not part of the revolution. Learners still need to do things, to have a sense of audience for, and feedback on, what they are doing, to feel personal progress, to be provoked and guided in their learning and to celebrate their own capabilities whilst also acknowledging those of others.

(Heppell and Ramondt, 1998: 26)

There is no need then to be confined by the values of a performative society, even technologically. However, it is unlikely that learner identity will be under threat in contexts where forms of learning include dialogic learning. Dialogic learning (Mezirow, 1981) occurs when insights and understandings emerge through dialogue in a learning environment. It is a form of learning where students draw upon their own experience to explain the concepts and ideas with which they are presented, and then use that experience to make sense for themselves and also to explore further issues. The promotion of such forms of learning can encourage students to critique and challenge the structures and boundaries within higher education and industry, whether virtual or terrestrial. This is because learning through dialogue brings to the fore, for students and tutors, the value of prior experience to current learning and thus can engage them in explorations and (re)constructions of learner identity.

With this in mind, it should also be acknowledged that problem-based learning, for some, can put learner identity in jeopardy because of the ways in which it can disturb students' understandings of what counts as knowledge and what it means to be a learner. For example, students' perceptions of themselves and the ways in which they learn most effectively can be contested through working and learning in a group. Here, students are often challenged to consider the role of their experience in learning and to examine the relationship between prior experience and understandings in relation to propositional knowledge. Propositional knowledge is the kind of knowledge that for some time has been seen as that which includes discipline-based theories and concepts derived from bodies of knowledge, practical principles and generalizations, and specific propositions about particular cases, decisions or actions (Eraut, 1994). However, the continual development of new knowledge and new types of knowledge means that the borders between kinds of knowledge are always on the move. Therefore it is not only difficult for students to explore what might count as knowledge, but also that in the face of so much new knowledge there is still, as Eraut has suggested, a risk of students accepting propositional knowledge provided by tutors in ways that are uncritical and unquestioning. Students whose learner identity is threatened by the idea that knowledge is not certain and that there are different ways of knowing, may experience conflict and dissonance. Such challenges for students about what counts as valid knowledge, and the more difficult problem of who makes the decisions about what counts as valid knowledge, can be a threat or a benefit in the process of the development and understanding of learner identity.

For the most part problem-based learning would seem to offer many students the opportunity of (re)discovering their learner identity by learning to 'make sense' for themselves. The result is that problem-based learning can go some way to helping students to understand their situations and frameworks and thus present opportunities for personal and pedagogical shifts to take place in their lives.

Learning context

The notion of the learning context is not new and has been discussed in a variety of ways by authors who have predominantly been concerned with students' learning experiences. For example, Ramsden (1984, 1992) suggested that students' perception of the learning context is an integral component of their learning. The learning context is created through students' experience of the constituents of the programmes on which they are studying, namely teaching methods, assessment mechanisms and the overall design of the curriculum. Ramsden suggests that students respond to the situation they perceive, which may differ from that which has been defined by educators. Yet often, however much it is denied, educators tend to think of learning contexts as static environments. Each year the programme or module on offer is usually fairly similar to the one offered last year and so students are taught in the same way with the same material. It is as if people, and students in particular, are put into contexts and watched while they move about inside them. Yet learning contexts are transient in nature, and much of the real learning that takes place for students occurs beyond the parameters of the presented material. Furthermore, Taylor (1986) has argued that since educational programmes are temporary environments, it is important to raise students' awareness of the changing nature of the learning environment, peers and tutors, and themselves within it. Therefore, recognition of students' perceptions of the formal learning context is key to facilitating students' ability to manage learning effectively.

I would argue that the concept of learning context incorporates more than just the students' experience of the component's teaching methods, assessment mechanisms and the overall design of the curriculum. Equally, learning context comprises more than that which can be defined according to the situation and perhaps even the disciplinary area of study. What I am proposing is a notion of learning context that incorporates the interplay of all the values, beliefs, relationships, frameworks and external structures that operate within a given learning environment. For example, I am arguing for a notion of learning context that is broader than students' experiences of the curriculum and teaching methods in which they are engaged, but a conception that acknowledges the values that underpin those structures, the values that staff and students bring to that context and the relationships that occur (or fail to occur) between students, and between staff and students. Learning context also incorporates the way in which the curriculum is situated within the university and the broader framework of higher education, thereby affecting what it means to be a learner in those contexts. Furthermore, the notion of learning context does not only comprise the formal curriculum but also the informal one – the one students create for themselves. For example, recent research into students' work and leisure time beyond the formal boundaries of the curriculum raised an interesting concern: students involved in problem-based learning programmes chose to spend such large amounts of time undertaking research and studying, that tutors became concerned about the way in which the learning was impinging upon their social life (Savin-Baden, 1996; Deadman, 1998). This might suggest that the smallest component of any learning context could be said to be the formal curriculum, since the learning context is in reality rarely bounded by formal structures but instead by those who comprise and define it.

To shift away from a notion of learning context that is characterized by the formal structures of a higher education environment, and to move towards a view of learning context that incorporates informal learning opportunities and broader systemic issues, raises a number of concerns about the concept of transferable skills. Transferable skills are expected to be applicable across different contexts, for example learned in the university and transferred to the world of work. Yet there needs to be a distinction made between transferable skills and the ability of transferring skills. Bridges (1993) has argued that transferable skills are those which it is supposed can be deployed in a variety of settings with little or no adaptation – such as word processing skills. Yet some skills are more context dependent (for example, the ability to negotiate) and require of the students more adaptation to the context than the simpler transferable skills such as word processing. Such adaptation demands meta-skills, because students are required to adjust and apply their skills to different situations and social contexts. He concluded by saying

> These begin to look like very sophisticated personal/intellectual achievements, which might explain why they are not in abundant supply . . . they look more like the kind of competence, capability or ability which lies at the heart of the sensitive, responsive and adaptable exercise of professionalism in any sphere than the atomistic list of 'competencies' towards which we are sometimes invited to direct our enthusiasm.
>
> (Bridges, 1993: 51)

Many curricula today include transferable skills as part of the undergraduate programme, particularly in professional curricula. Courses in professional education have been the single highest growth area in UK higher education, due to the incorporation of professions such as nursing, occupational therapy and physiotherapy into the university system. This, along with the increasing links with industry, has meant that there has been an assumption that formal learning contexts can offer students opportunities to develop skills that are immediately transferable from the academic context to the work context. There is a question too about where it is that students find the ability to do the transferring; perhaps it is the informal context such as the debates in the coffee bars and through practising presentation skills in their flats at the weekend.

There is a complex interface between the formal learning contexts of university, fieldwork education and industrial placements. Students in professional education often have a practice placement component with their degree where they spend a number of weeks in work-based environments learning with practitioners. The difference between the kinds of learning that take place during placements compared with the kinds of learning that take place in university are rarely articulated by staff, students and practitioners. This is not just because of the different understandings of what is important within those contexts, such as what students know and can theorize about compared with what they can apply and undertake. It is also because of the way in which academics and practitioners tend to emphasize differences rather than seek to engage with similarities. For example, we tend to set academic writing, such as essays, against report writing undertaken in a practical setting; likewise we set skills practised on campus against 'doing it in real life'. There may be differences, but imposing a notion of forms of knowledge or types of skills that set up learning in university as something so remarkably different from learning on fieldwork will only help the student towards a deeper and unnecessary understanding of the colossal barriers that we ourselves have erected. This is not to deny that there are differences, but forms of problem-based learning, which equip students to value the use of theory in practice contexts and the use of anecdote and biography in academic contexts, can enable students to contextualize knowledge and skills, both within and across contexts. Yet in our quest to understand the kinds of learning which are similar between practical and academic contexts we must also remember that issues and challenges that emerge in different kinds of context also tend to collide with matters connected with people's lives, people's relationships with one another and the ways in which they 'learn in relation' to one another.

Learning in relation

'Learning in relation' (after Weil, 1989) is used here to capture the idea that students learning with and through others in ways that help to make connections between their lives, with other subjects and disciplines and with personal concerns, offers students particular kinds of learning opportunities. For example, while students may learn in lectures or in group work, they may also learn through discussion in common rooms and as they debate the material with which they have just been presented while walking between lectures.

This kind of informal learning may occur somewhat incidentally, but for many students there is often a desire to make sense of their learning in relation to their lives and experiences – both in terms of prior learning and current experiences, as well as with the experiences of significant others, peers and tutors. Weil's study, which explored the perspectives of adults who had returned to higher education to undertake a course after an interval of over five years, sought to understand how their prior learning impacted upon their expectations and experiences of returning to a formal context. Weil suggested that for the women in her study the idea of a context that did not allow for 'learning in relation' was something that put their self-esteem at risk. For example, these women spoke of needing to make connections with their lives, prior experience, other disciplines and issues that mattered personally. When they were not able or allowed to make such connections, there was a sense of fragility, so that their ability to value their own perspectives and speak for themselves was at risk. Opportunities to 'learn in relation' offered these women freedom to develop a sense of trust in their own voice: 'without feeling that powerful forces would intervene either to silence that voice, tell it it was *wrong*, or revive the feeling that to speak, to write, to create and to have access to knowledge in higher education was not really "for the likes of them"' (Weil, 1989: 130). The notion of voice in the learning process is central to 'learning in relation' since it is through students' ability to speak for themselves and to find and use their voice, that they are able to articulate what it means to 'learn in relation' to their lives. For example, interacting with others in a learning situation becomes a key component of 'learning in relation' since it is through dialogue within a given context that students begin to make sense of concepts for themselves. Working and learning with others offers students opportunities to explore their own perspectives as well as those of their peers. In particular, working in groups can help students to become effective researchers of information, who work as a team to learn to explore and critique material together. 'Learning in relation', therefore, is a concept that incorporates not just the idea that students learn, as it were, in relation to their own knowledge and experience, but also to that of others. Learning such as this can prompt support and encouragement that may further group and individual motivation. For example, students 'make sense' not just in terms of their goals, but also in terms of their relationships and how they interact with others. Thus it is essential that students are encouraged to become active participants in their learning and decision making, and are enabled to create and establish legitimacy for group debate and action.

Barnett (1994) has suggested that higher education is necessarily a process of becoming and argued for a process of education in which the student can be 'released into herself': Barnett sees this 'being released' not in terms of empowerment, self-realization or emancipation, but in terms of constructing 'their own voice'. What Barnett essentially appears to argue for is the development of a learner identity through which the learner is able not only to construct (and presumably deconstruct) and articulate her own perspective in her own way, but also to be able to defend this perspective before peers and authorities. In essence what we see here is the interaction of learner identity with 'learning in relation' whereby learner histories also impinge on current experience, as well as the contexts in which students are learning. Therefore, what a learner brings to a context in terms of their identity and their desire to learn in relation will necessarily affect that context.

Out of sight, out of mind?

The question then remains, why are the elements of learner identity, learning contexts and 'learning in relation' important to learning – and, in particular, to problem-based learning contexts? These elements, when taken together, are concepts that can affect the expectations and the understandings of what it means to learn in higher education. These elements are important for three reasons, all of which go some way to preventing the performative slide. Taken together, they enable staff and students to see that curricula which just focus on what students can do, are not in fact able to equip students to be questioning practitioners of the future. Creating professionals of the future who have unquestioning and uncritical perspectives and practices reduces the possibility for developing effective professionals with self-understanding who can cope with uncertainty and challenge taken-for-granted practices.

The first reason that these elements are important is that through them it is possible to acknowledge and value the inner world of the learner. To recognize and centralize these elements within curricula will mean that knowledge and self will be engaged in ways that enable learners to connect their learning with their prior experiences, with issues and problems that matter to them personally. Performative practices that focus only on what students are able to do will not be possible, because there will not be a separation of the outer discourse from the inner discourse resulting in a chasm between the 'knower and what is known' (Bernstein, 1996: 87). Knower and what is known will be inseparable.

The second reason is that the realization of these missing elements, in the context of the life of the learner, will enable the gap to be bridged between the formal and the informal learning context. Students tend to see the world beyond the university as a stable entity thus, for instance, industry and the health service are, these days, seen as given, and indeed often seen by students as the places where right answers are to be found. Yet if these three elements are focused upon in undergraduate and preregistration curricula, and students are encouraged to engage with them, then students will realize that the structures and frameworks of the external world are to be critiqued as deeply as any knowledge with which they are presented. As a result students' learner identities will not emerge from pedagogic identities developed through the tug of war between the academic world and the world of work. Instead they may seek to transcend both worlds through critique and reframing knowledge, skills, practices and cultures for themselves.

This in turn, which is the final point here, will result in a different kind of student – not one who has been created through societal agendas and performative or disciplinary academic values, but one who has constructed herself. Finding and using their voice can enable students to see learning as more than the accumulation of a body of knowledge or the acquisition of particular work related competencies. Thus we see that these elements are vital to the building and sustaining of a kind of higher education that can equip and enable students with more than a pedagogic identity defined and developed through the trends of the current age. Although this may seem idealistic, there are learners who say that this is their experience. Simultaneously there are curricula in which issues of learner identity, learning context and 'learning in relation' are prone to being omitted from curricular discourse for any or all of the following reasons:

- The shift away from collective forms of learning, such as group work and seminars, to individualistic forms of learning characterized by solitary and therefore necessarily self-centred learning contexts.
- Forms of assessment that support and sustain the belief that there exist sound bodies of knowledge, right answers and correct performative practices rather than the challenging and transcending of frameworks, both practical and theoretical.
- The shift to mass higher education, which is resulting in increasingly varied and fragmented student experiences, that in the long term may result in student dissatisfaction through unrealized expectations.
- The growth in the 'market' of higher education, which is currently, and no doubt will continue to be, increasingly subject to the demands and caprice of industry as well as the wider society as they become greater stakeholders paying for their goods in the market-place.
- The shift to students as consumers who seek to demand their consumer rights (under the Trades Description Act?) in the form of acquiring the relevant competencies for their chosen careers. Students are also more likely to be attracted to those institutions which are more 'high-tech' than those that are not, because they may offer them quality with convenience.

To some extent it could be argued that the reasons that these three elements of learner identity, learning context and 'learning in relation' are omitted in many approaches to teaching and learning today is because of the disparities between what is espoused by staff compared with the realities of the lived curriculum. For example, Weil discovered that learner identity conflicts arose from:

> aspects of experience related to gender, race, and/or class being made invisible or being re-defined on 'tutors' terms'. The intensity of their impact, however, seemed to be heightened when coupled with other contradictions between teachers' espoused and actual behaviours . . . Feelings of dissonance and conflict were also enhanced by course structures and pedagogic practices which actively discouraged the mutual

exchange of knowledge and experience, and the critical evaluation of competing perspectives.

(Weil, 1986: 231)

Given the changes in higher education and the incoherence of the overall experience of students in a mass system of higher education, it would seem that the omissions relate not only to what is going on inside the curriculum but also to the external pressures pushing towards performativity and 'infotainment' (Ritzer, 1996) in the context of a higher education system in crisis.

Conclusion

The important issues of learner identity, learning context and 'learning in relation', need to be realized as vital components in curricula, which seek to address the performative slide. In particular, the elements are core ingredients when adopting the kind of problem-based learning that centres around dialogic learning, and put discourse and relationship centre stage. This argument will be built on further in the subsequent chapter and supported in later chapters in the context of research. However, if problem-based learning is to become a dominant mode in higher education, then an exploration of the ways it is played out in practice is required.

Part 2

Problem-based Learning:
An Unarticulated Subtext?

Part 2

Understanding the young and
technologically connected

3

Games of Chess

Introduction

This chapter presents four short curricular case studies that demonstrate the multidimensional nature of problem-based learning within different disciplines and educational environments. The notion of different forms of problem-based learning captured through the image of games of chess was developed through my experience of undertaking research within problem-based learning contexts in which there were different curricula models that utilized components of the problem-based learning process in diverse ways. Some of the issues and concerns that were apparent emerged from conflicts experienced by staff and students, which arose from the relationship between learning and prior experiences, the interaction of staff and students, and the association between the curriculum and professional practice. This chapter describes the interaction of competing agendas for staff and students within the four programmes, and the ways in which professional and institutional agendas affected how problem-based learning occurred in practice. It should be remembered that what is presented here must be seen as a number of snapshots of what was taking place within these curricula over a relatively short period of time, and that contexts change and move even as research is undertaken within them.

Research design

The research was undertaken in four distinct professional groups in different departments in four British universities, from 1991 to 1995. Each department had implemented problem-based learning in some way but all differed in their approach to its use. The choice of sites was guided by my desire to explore four diverse professional areas that were using problem-based learning in different ways.

The methodology adopted was qualitative and was both emergent and collaborative in its design and process. The research design needed to allow for the idiosyncrasy of human action and experience. Through it I wanted to be able to build on collaborative relationships with the participants of the enquiry, invite reflexivity and critique, and encourage negotiation of meaning beyond the descriptive level. Initially I felt the naturalistic paradigm would allow me to participate in the world of the individual so as to understand and make sense of problem-based learning as it was experienced and understood by those involved in problem-based learning programmes. As the study progressed I used methods that were predominantly associated with new paradigm research (Reason and Rowan, 1981), since a central concern of the research was to illuminate people and their lives as three-dimensional, not as subjects without a history or a future. In practice this meant I moved away from questions about how decisions were made and implemented in problem-based learning programmes, and questions about how groups worked and whether assessments fitted with the ethos of problem-based learning. Instead I sought to know people in their contexts, and to understand how they saw themselves and their experiences in relation to problem-based learning. I also attempted to explore the ways in which individual and personal concerns were affected by public issues such as professional accountability, competence to practice and higher education spending cuts. Thus, I began to try to make sense of and bring to the fore other dimensions of experience that affected and were affected by the contexts in which problem-based learning was occurring.

One-to-one in-depth interviews were used throughout the study as the method of data collection, as well as informal discussion with both groups and individuals, group interviews, and analysis of course documents. A diverse group of staff and students were formally interviewed over a three year period and data were explored and discussed further over the subsequent year. Interviews lasted between one and two hours. Multiple methods and data sources along with a systematic interpretation of areas of convergence and contradiction were used in order to develop an understanding of different sorts of knowing in diverse contexts. One of the central difficulties with multisite studies is the decision about how to structure the data in ways that portray what people claimed for and sought in problem-based learning within the learning culture they were experiencing. For example, there was a question of whether to write across the sites by focusing on key themes or to aim for depth and complexity by keeping data within single sites. Alternatively, I could have combined the two approaches by interpreting data within the context of each site and then include a discrete consideration of cross-site issues. I did not not want to lose complexity by generalizing findings across the sites nor did I want a repetitive and comparative single site approach. MacLure and Marr (1988) argued that the analytic framework applied to interview data derives from work in the analysis of discourse, and resists the construction of categories that abstract talk from its conversational context. To give an example:

rather than collecting all expressions of, say, 'commitment' or 'idealism' in the interview, and then trying to identify the common meanings in these categories, across all teachers, a discourse-based approach
would ask how such notions as commitment and idealism are used by
different teachers to make particular points, to defend particular views
or actions, to claim particular moral stances.

(MacLure and Marr, 1988: 5)

Through using a discourse-based approach such as this, I was able to structure the data across the sites in ways that demonstrated complexity but that
also offered, as it were, a structural coherence in the form of a framework
for understanding staff and students' experiences of problem-based learning. Before this framework is introduced I will set out the context of the
research through the presentation of the four curricula case studies:

Gimmer University[1]

Gimmer University was a traditional university with a reputation for academic excellence. The problem-based learning course ran alongside convention-
ally taught modules in the third year of a BSc in mechanical engineering,
which was accredited by the Institute of Mechanical Engineers who provided
exemption from the professional examination. As the problem-based learning
module was a small optional component of the degree it was not affected or
constrained by the professional body.

The introduction of problem-based learning at Gimmer

Problem-based learning replaced a conventional lecture-based module on
vibration that occurred in the third year of the traditional degree programme.
The problem-based learning module was designed to promote a move away
from the transmission of technical content and to enable students to develop skills in using new and previously learned material to engage with real
engineering problem situations. As the course was an optional third year
module it had to conform to the existing course structure, which meant fit-
ting it into the overall timetable of 30 contact hours over 20 weeks. Problem-
based learning was introduced into this particular module because in the
past students had tended to avoid examination questions requiring problem-
solving abilities and the application of content to problems in ways that were
essential to engineering practice. It was also introduced because the module
tutor felt that within the original lecture-based vibration module there was
too much emphasis on technical theory and too little on its practical application. The aims were written to reflect a move away from the transmission
of a body of knowledge towards the development of professional skills, and
the capacity to solve or manage real problems and present effective answers.

The course in practice

Before the problem-based learning module commenced, the students attended an introductory session that was designed to help them to choose whether to take the course as one of their third year options. On average, 30 students made that choice. The module comprised six problem situations, which were dealt with in three pairs, each pair phase lasting six or seven weeks. The problem situations were organized in this way so that each group of students engaged with one problem situation acted as consultants and considered the other in the role of clients. The 'consultant' students were required to hand in a group report offering their solution.

As clients, the students had to devise their own criteria to evaluate the issues of the other problem situation so that they could assess the consultant group's answer and report effectively. Having read that report they then prepared a brief critique of it. At the end of each phase oral presentations took place with a staff member present. These took the form of a meeting during which one group represented the consultant and the other the client; the roles were then reversed for the second problem. This pattern was then repeated to cover the further two pairs of problems.

Students worked in groups of three or four and could choose with whom to work. They were organized into groups primarily to reduce time spent by individual students on preparing the reports and working out the calculations, and also to reduce staff input by enabling staff to meet with groups rather than individuals. Group work was also adopted to encourage students to cooperate and learn from one another, which mirrored professional life where cooperation was the norm. Neither facilitators nor rooms were allocated for group work. Each group chose when and where to meet and worked independently on how to present its work in the presentation sessions. The module was coordinated by two staff members, and assisted by a third. The staff who provided some seminars were also available for tutorials at the students' request.

Students were assessed on three written consultant reports, three written client reports, oral presentations of these six reports and one answer to a question on a particular topic. More weight, in terms of marks, was given to the later problems because the earlier problems were designed to be more formative. Students were given a group mark for the reports with some individual weighting on the oral presentations. There was also a test at the end of the module, which was designed to check the individual's grasp of the basic principles of the subject.

Lembert University

Lembert University was a former polytechnic with a bias towards professional education. The B.Eng in Automotive Design (AMD) Engineering was a four year sandwich course with the first year common with a B.Eng mechanical engineering degree. The approach in years two and four of the course was problem-based learning, the third year being the industrial placement.

Automotive design education in context

There has been increasing criticism of engineering design and designers in the UK and the shortcomings were believed to be handicapping the UK's competitiveness in the markets for manufactured goods. In the late 1980s the then Department of Education and Science encouraged innovation in this area and particularly the introduction of studio-based degrees that had strength in design teaching. In response to these issues raised by the government, experts in industry were consulted regarding the need for a course that would centre around mechanical engineering design, focusing on products of the automotive industry. The problem-based curriculum was developed, with the aim that the course would encourage students to develop engineering design skills synonymous with those required in professional practice. The course was designed by first identifying detailed intentions that stated the skills, knowledge and general characteristics of a designer. It was this set of intentions that led to the choice of problem-based learning. To ensure that these goals were achieved the assessment was directly linked with course objectives that emerged from the set of intentions.

The course in practice

The specific automotive engineering aspects of the course were only introduced in the second year that centred around problem-based learning. Prior to this students had experienced a traditional lecture-based approach to learning, either on the joint first year of the mechanical engineering/ automotive engineering degree or externally through undertaking a Higher National Diploma (HND), or equivalent qualification. Thus, for most students the conventional pattern of previous learning comprised lectures, practicals and unseen exams.

This problem-based learning course had 18 students undertaking it, predominantly white British males, with a mixture of working and middle-class, mature students and 18-year-olds. The course has since expanded to take over 30 students per annum. Eight staff in total were involved in various components of this course. Initially students were introduced to problem-based learning, an experiential learning cycle (based on Kolb and Fry, 1975) and the notion of a learning journal in which they were expected to record their reflections on learning. Students received a course guide that explained the rationale, objectives and content of the course. The course was structured around a series of modules that, although predominantly discipline based, overlapped because of the nature of problem scenarios that students were expected to resolve. For example, in designing a suspension system in solid mechanics students would also be expected to incorporate facets of basic car design.

Students worked in groups of four or five and could choose with whom to work for some of the problems that were set, but were allocated to groups for others; this largely depended on the tutor who had provided the problem scenario. The pace at which new problems were introduced depended on the level of students' understanding rather than a fixed timetable. Students' level of understanding was ascertained by members of staff teaching particular modules through informal group discussion with students. Lecturing was included in the course but was limited to information that was required to engage with a given problem, and consequently did not fit into any form of schedule. The students had a design studio allocated for their sole use and could work in the room from 9 am to 9 pm. Each group worked independently and did not have a facilitator, but did have access to the members of staff who had set the problems.

Students were assessed by continuous assessment methods through various types of problem scenarios that were set by the members of staff for each module. The scenarios varied in their demands from model making to open-ended design projects. The problem scenarios set were generally group based although there were also individual projects and an individual final year project. In the problem-based work each group presented their solution orally and handed in a report prepared by the group as a whole. Self-assessment and peer assessment were used to enable students to identify individual and group skills and attitudes. Tutor assessment formed the major component of the assessment process. Additionally, students were expected to keep a log book and learning journal which were also assessed. Assessment was carried out against criteria taken from the detailed course objectives.

Baslow University

Baslow was a former Institute of Higher Education, which first gained Polytechnic status and then later became a University. The nursing programme at Baslow has experienced a number of changes in recent years. For example in 1990, following permission being refused to commence a Project 2000 programme (Project 2000 set out important changes in the way that nurses were to be educated), a diploma course was implemented that had only two intakes. In 1991 the Project 2000 degree commenced, that consequently occurred in tandem with the diploma course. It was during this process of change that it was decided to include problem-based learning in the degree programme.

Nursing education in context

Nurse training in the past was typically carried out in nursing schools or colleges attached to hospitals. Student nurses were classed as part of the NHS at an apprenticeship level. The professional body decided to make major changes in the structure of training and saw the role of higher education as crucial in this. It set out its proposal in a document named Project 2000 that had far reaching structural implications for the profession. The first Project 2000 course began in 1989 with the first trained nurses qualifying from it in 1992. As a result, both nursing courses and the profession had been experiencing a period of change, moving away from the apprenticeship model of learning that had been in place for decades, towards learning that took place in the context of higher education. Nursing courses in England were validated by the English National Board (ENB) as a representative body of the United Kingdom Central Council (UKCC) that was concerned with the registration of nurses.

The introduction of problem-based learning at Baslow

The three year degree course was divided into two components: the common foundation programme and the branch programme. These two components were consecutive, lasted 18 months each and were each three semesters in length. Within this structure students spent a total of 72 weeks on clinical practice over the three year degree programme. Within the common foundation programme 20 weeks were spent in clinical practice in the form of five four-week periods in the major areas of nursing practice. During these five periods students returned to campus for one problem-based learning day each week. Campus weeks comprised traditional lectures and some practical workshops. The staff/student contact time was very high, with students being timetabled for over 20 hours per week.

In planning the degree programme, course designers decided that it would be a useful activity for students to return to the university from clinical practice for one day each week. These days were initially discussed and planned during course design meetings as reflective days, but later documented in the course submission document as both a reflective and a problem-based learning day. In reality it was decided to use problem-based learning methods during this one day on campus during clinical practice weeks, since problem-based learning was seen by staff to incorporate reflection.

Staff felt it vital that degree students became as self-directed as possible during the common foundation programme (the first 18 months of the course) and they felt that problem-based learning would enable this to occur. Staff saw the difference between a diploma student and a degree student as being rooted in the way in which students acquired and used their knowledge. Degree students were seen to be able to learn how to learn for themselves.

The course in practice

There were 30 students undertaking the course, predominantly white British females, a mixture of school leavers and mature students. Six of the students were training to be midwives and four students were undertaking the mental health branch of the programme. Neither of these groups took part in problem-based learning. The rest of the cohort were training to be registered general nurses and were all involved in the problem-based learning component of the course. The course used problem-based learning to facilitate reflection one day a week, and it was designed to be centred around problems and issues that occurred to students while they were in the clinical environment. Students were given, in advance of their placements, a log book that contained topic areas for each week and included a profile of the different facets of the topic about which the students could collect data. Students were expected to generate their own problem scenarios from issues that arose from their experience of clinical practice, but which also fitted within a designated area defined by the tutor. For example, students may be provided with a subject such as 'the concept of care' as the topic for one week. They were then expected to consider this concept whilst on clinical practice and subsequently return to campus with a problem scenario that they had experienced and that related to the given topic.

The students worked in groups of six or seven for the day. They were allocated to these groups and had a facilitator with them at the beginning and the end of the day. The groups initially comprised students who were all undertaking placements in differing clinical areas, but as the students objected to this they moved to work in groups where everyone was practising in the same or similar clinical areas. After the initial meeting students were given a 'problem sheet' that was designed to prompt them. They were then free to use the library or allocated rooms for the rest of the day. Students were expected to return at the end of the day to present their findings to the tutors and to the student body.

The problem-based component of the course was not assessed summatively, although students were expected to submit a folio of work they had completed that related to the problem-based learning days. Three members of staff were involved in this component; one member of staff had overall responsibility for designing and managing the problem-based learning day, and the two other members of staff acted as facilitators to the groups.

Stanage University

Stanage University was a high status British university. Within it a social work department offered a Diploma in Social Work (DipSW) that used problem-based learning as its underlying philosophy. Social work education experienced a period of change during the 1980s and through a debate between the Central Council for the Education and Training of Social

Workers (CCETSW), the employing agencies and the Department of Health, an uneasy compromise was reached in which all graduate courses were extended to two years and a new qualification – the DipSW – was introduced. The requirements for this qualification were expressed by CCETSW (CCETSW, 1989) in learning outcomes rather than programme content, which for some social work courses provided an opportunity for change.

The introduction of problem-based learning at Stanage

The change from a traditional academic curriculum to problem-based learning at Stanage was due to a number of reasons. First, there was curricular overload due to new material being introduced to add to existing material that was still felt to be relevant. There was difficulty in enabling students to make effective use of prior experience, and an associated problem was that many students perceived valid knowledge as that held exclusively by staff. A third reason was that students on social work courses often experienced difficulty applying theory to practice and tended to leave behind any theoretical knowledge they had acquired in their campus studies when they were on fieldwork placements.

Problem-based learning was introduced in order to address the above issues but also because the view was taken that working in small groups would provide stimulation and support from peers, a pool of experience on which to draw and opportunities for personal and professional development. It was thus expected that students would be prepared through this for working in professional teams. Problem-based learning was also introduced because it was felt that it was vital for students to learn strategies for problem analysis and intervention, and be motivated to continue to learn and acquire further skills, particularly in order to work effectively in a constantly changing society. The course aims, objectives and the problem scenarios were written to reflect all of these concerns.

The course in practice

At Stanage the social work curriculum consisted of five blocks that were spread over two years. The first, third and fifth block were based in the university, and the second and fourth in fieldwork placements. Problem-based learning took place primarily during campus studies and comprised a series of study units that increased in complexity through the course. The study units were developed from situations and problems derived from practice so that the theory studied on campus would be directly relevant to practice placements and to future experience as qualified social workers. The problem scenarios were designed to provide opportunities for learning to enable the students to reach the level of competence in the Statement of Requirements for the DipSW as set out in Paper 30 (CCETSW, 1989).

The two year diploma course attracted a variety of people, who defined themselves as working and middle class, and who were predominantly British and white. As it was a social work course all the students were at least 22 years of age on admission to it. Some students had first degrees, others had not and there tended to be a high proportion of non-graduate, working-class students. Problem-based learning essentially began from day one of the course, but before students were accepted on to the course they saw a video of problem-based learning 'in action', which was then discussed, so that they had some understanding of the type of course to which they were committing themselves. The course was in the process of expansion, so that there were 45 second year students and 75 first year students. Eight staff were also involved with the programme.

The students worked in groups of about ten and each group stayed together for the duration of the whole block, which was approximately ten weeks. There was a different study unit every two weeks and each unit comprised several (usually three) problem scenarios. Students were expected to tackle the work in the time available for the unit, which involved analysing each problem, exploring personal, ethical, social, legal and political dimensions.

Guided by a facilitator they established the skills, knowledge and understanding they had, then identified what skills they needed to learn and what knowledge they needed to acquire in order to work through the situation or problem. At the end of the block the groups were re-formed and students then worked through the next series of units. Each group was allocated a room in which to meet, and usually convened about three times each week. The students used resources such as videos, library facilities, departmental information and consultations with experts. There were also skills groups, one or two lectures per week, and one or two workshops per term on aspects such as discrimination. Students were assessed predominantly through essays that were done by them as individuals. Work that took place in the group, or which was done by the group, was not assessed.

Staff input comprised designing and planning study units, facilitating groups, and acting as consultants for particular topics and as personal tutors to students. In order to foster student autonomy and to be economical with human resources, the facilitator did not attend all the meetings, but would usually be present at the beginning and end of each unit.

Conclusion

This chapter has illustrated the ways in which problem-based learning can be implemented in diverse ways across different professions and institutional contexts. Internal and external influences on curricula, such as curricula constraints and the requirements of professional bodies can affect the ways in which problem-based learning might be implemented. This may be affected further by differences between staff's espoused intentions and their concerns about the way in which problem-based learning occurs in practice. Student experiences of problem-based learning, as revealed through data in the next chapters, reflect some of these complexities, but also relate to three particular interrelated concepts in students' lives. Thus, the framework of Dimensions of Learner Experience, presented in the next chapter, will convey the dynamics of incoherence, ambiguity and paradox in people's lives that emerged from being a learner in higher education and for some was prompted, it seemed, through a new and different way of learning.

Note

1. The research sites were named after rock faces where I climb.

4

From Rooks, Pawns and Bishops

Introduction

At each of the research sites there was a diversity of opinion about how problem-based learning might be understood. By examining experiences of this approach across different institutions and educational environments, it became possible to point to differing ideologies and purposes, as well as differences between what was espoused and what occurred in practice at the different sites. Yet diversity can bring with it a conceptual richness that reaches far beyond concerns about narrow definitions of problem-based learning, whether groups should comprise six or eight members and what might constitute the role of the tutor in this process. These kinds of concerns can often get in the way of dialogue in the implementation and enactment of problem-based learning as well as of helping students to see the value of relationship in the learning process. Gergen (1987) has argued that the discourse of relationship represents a 'vastly unarticulated subtext', and has suggested that in articulating this subtext it is 'as if we have at our disposal a rich language for characterizing rooks, pawns and bishops but have yet to discover the game of chess' (Gergen, 1987: 63). Issues such as group size and tutor roles may be termed the rooks, pawns and bishops – disparate pieces in a game of chess. As such this chapter moves away from the pieces and examine the nature of experience in the context of problem-based learning programmes. The focus of this chapter is the presentation of the principal components of a new framework for understanding the nature of learner experience on problem-based learning programmes, which arose from my cross-site investigation into problem-based learning. This chapter offers an overview of the overarching framework that emerged from the data whilst the next chapter demonstrates, through students' data, the complexities and transitions experienced by students in the four problem-based learning contexts.

I have termed this framework 'Dimensions of Learner Experience' to encapsulate the idea that learners do not just engage the pedagogical components of themselves in learning. Students do not simply learn the thing they are studying at the time, they also learn about people, contexts, likes and dislikes, and most importantly themselves. Learning is not a linear process whereby students who are engaged in learning are just thinking about that subject, in that context, at that particular time. Learning is about engaging different dimensions of ourselves in the learning process. Emotions and feelings are often the ones that are most neglected in learning, and it seems, at times, that there is almost a prohibition about them intruding into educational environments. This framework offers a way of seeing learning as something which is not, as Dewey (1938) argued, marked by the opposition between the idea that education is something which is developed from within *or* from without. Instead the framework seeks rather to embrace the ideal of a multifaceted learner with diverse experience, both internal and external, where interaction of the various components of the learning self necessarily affect one another.

The framework

Dimensions of Learner Experience emerged from my empirical study, as described in Chapter 3, that sought to explore staff's and students' experiences of problem-based learning across disciplines and educational environments. What was evident at the outset was that students were offered, through problem-based learning, opportunities to value their prior learning experiences and to develop an independence in enquiry, opportunities that many had been denied through the didactic methods of teaching which they had experienced in the past. It also seemed that problem-based learning was an approach to learning that could accommodate new political, economic, educational and professional concerns, whilst also being a means of managing scarce resources, coping with a larger and more diverse student group, making education vocationally more relevant and bringing learning rather than teaching to the fore. However, there has been little research in the UK that has explored staff's and students' experiences of problem-based learning. What emerged from the research and the subsequent process of data interpretation was a means of structuring data through three concepts which captured complexity and paradox across the sites. I have termed these concepts: personal stance, pedagogical stance and interactional stance. These three interrelated sets of concepts emerged from people's experience of problem-based learning as revealed through data, and together they encapsulated a multifaceted view of learner experience. The stances are defined briefly as follows:

- Personal stance: the way in which staff and students see themselves in relation to the learning context and give their own distinctive meaning to their experience of that context.
- Pedagogical stance: the ways in which people see themselves as learners in particular educational environments.

- Interactional stance: the ways in which learners work and learn in groups and construct meaning in relation to one another.

Stance is used here in the sense of one's attitude, belief or disposition towards a particular context, person or experience. It refers to a particular position one takes up in life towards something, at a particular point in time. The term 'stance' has been adopted because it reflects the idea that a person has made some form of choice, they have developed a stance towards something, whether consciously or unconsciously. Stance is not just a matter of attitude, it encompasses our unconscious beliefs and prejudices, our prior learning experiences, our perceptions of tutors, peers and learning situations, and our past, present and future selves. The stances emerged from students' accounts of learning through problem-based learning. Students spoke of their experiences of problem-based learning predominantly in terms of the ways they saw themselves in relation to the learning context, their views of themselves as learners, and their relationships with peers. Hence personal, pedagogical and interactional stances have been used to denote these inter-related concepts. Although these concepts overlap in a variety of ways, the stances are discussed as separate entities within this chapter. Each stance contains within it a number of interrelated concepts, referred to as 'domains', which relate to the overarching concept of the stance as a whole. The term 'domain' is used here to denote the overlapping spheres within each stance and it was chosen to reflect the notion that there are particular locations within each of the stances between which a person may move. However, the borders of the domains merge with one another and therefore shifts between domains are transitional areas where particular kinds of learning occurs.

Transitional learning

Transitional learning is learning that occurs as a result of critical reflection upon shifts (transitions) that have taken place for the students personally (including viscerally) pedagogically and/or interactionally. Transition is used here to denote shifts in learner experience caused by a challenge to the person's life-world. The concept of life-world is taken from Habermas (1989) and represents the idea that as human beings we have a culturally transmitted stock of taken-for-granted perspectives and interpretations that are organized in a communicative way. Thus, challenges to students' life-world(s) may be at odds with, or bear little relationship to, their current meaning systems, so ultimately prompting transitions in their lives. Transitions occur in particular areas of students' lives, at different times and in distinct ways. The notion of transitions carries with it the idea of movement from one place to another and with it the necessity of taking up a new position in a different place. Critical reflection often occurred during research interviews, in discussions of critical incidents with students or in the context of group work. What was important about the critical reflection was not just that it *did* occur but the way in which it afforded students the opportunity to discuss both the quality of the learning experience and the ways in which they had managed transitions. Thus, through this process, what could have become merely anecdotal reminiscence for many students, became the means by which students were enabled to make sense of and to manage the learning that had occurred during and as a result of the transitions.

Students who have made a transition from one domain to another no longer see the previous domain in quite the same way, and as such will need to make sense of their current domain through reflecting upon the past domain and giving meaning to the learning that has taken place. In transitional learning self-development is not necessarily a process of change towards higher levels of existence, but instead movement is seen as a shift away from the learner's current way of understanding.

Transitional learning is often prompted by *disjunction*. Disjunction (after Jarvis, 1987; Weil, 1989) is used here to refer to a sense of fragmentation of part of, or all of the self, characterized by frustration and confusion, and a loss of sense of self, which often results in anger and the need for right answers. The very nature of disjunction means that managing it presents a challenge to the individual, which in turn may result in disjunction being seen as something negative and undesirable. Yet in many ways disjunction can be dynamic; dynamic in the sense that both enabling and disabling forms of disjunction may lead to transitions in students' lives. Disjunction is often the starting point for learning (Jarvis, 1987), but for many students it may not *only* occur in relation to learning that is seen to be relevant and meaningful. Disjunction may occur because, through problem-based learning, students experience challenges to their life-world. What also emerged from the students' data were the ways in which disjunction could be disabling or enabling in nature. Disabling disjunction occurred when students encountered a challenge to their life-world that resulted in an increased sense of disjunction and when they felt unable to react in ways which would help them to make greater sense of their situation and lives. Enabling disjunction occurred when students were able to shift away from feeling stuck in learning and were able to find and engage with new meanings and perspectives. It is important to note that the same challenge to two students can result in enabling disjunction for one and disabling disjunction for another. This is because of the way in which the disjunction experienced relates to an individual's life-world. Whenever a transition occurs, be it within a domain or across a domain boundary, there will always be a changed sense of disjunction.

Although the type of disjunction differed for individual students, there were some general trends. The institutional culture and the relationship between problem-based learning and other components of the curriculum affected the extent to which disabling disjunction occurred. For example, problem-based learning did not appear to fit and work well in 'traditional' institutions that were set up for lecture-based learning, since the environment and the attitudes of staff caused a barrier to its acceptance. Thus, there appeared to be a greater potential for disabling disjunction to occur within students' pedagogical stances for those experiencing problem-based learning as a component of a traditional programme.

An overview of the framework of Dimensions of Learner Experience

The framework of Dimensions of Learner Experience comprises three stances: personal stance, pedagogical stance and interactional stance. The stances are as shown in Figure 4.1.

To recap: each stance contains a number of domains and movement between them is diverse, depending on each individual and set of circumstances. The borders of the domains are somewhat blurred, as in the edges of colours in the spectrum. Movement can also take place within domains as well as across them.

Personal stance

My use of the term, personal stance, follows Salmon:

> Taking the metaphor of personal stance gives a different meaning, not just to learning, but also to teaching, which, as teachers, we think about less often than we should. Because personal stance refers to the positions which each of us takes up in life, this metaphor emphasizes aspects of experience which go deeper than the merely cognitive, and which reflect its essentially relational, social and agentic character.
>
> (Salmon, 1989: 231)

The term personal stance is used here to depict the way in which staff and students see themselves in relation to the learning context and give their own distinctive meaning to their experience of that context. Personal stance encompasses the means by which they discover, define and place themselves within the problem-based learning environment and express the interplay

Figure 4.1   The three stances of Dimensions of Learner Experience

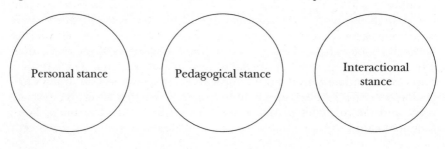

between what they bring to, and take from, their learning experiences. The ways in which people speak about themselves, view their profession, their peers, the facilitator and the institution are explored within the conceptual framework of personal stance.

To talk of people having a personal stance is often to assume that people *know* the nature of their own personal stance. Yet students did not use the phrase 'personal stance' but instead spoke of themselves in terms of the relationship between their learning, their personal biographies and the higher education context in which they were being taught. When students spoke of issues that I would associate with the notion of personal stance, they spoke of their particular view of the world and the way that view had been challenged or changed through some catalyst within the learning context. Catalysts varied according to students' circumstances, and particular features and dynamics of the learning context, about which they felt differently at different times and which often prompted transitions in learning.

Transitions in students' personal stances were often sites of struggle. Transitions were sometimes difficult and disturbing; yet in many cases they were places where personal change took place. For example, for some students the marked difference between their prior learning experiences and their experience of problem-based learning produced conflict about the nature of personal responsibility within a learning context. During prior learning experiences some had come to equate 'taking responsibility' with learning right answers as defined by teachers. In problem-based learning taking responsibility often meant identifying personal learning needs and fulfilling those needs. Personal change often took place when students were able to accept and make the shift from authority centred learning to learning that related to their own needs as learners. Thus shifts within students' personal stances could change according to the learning context and according to students' self perceptions at particular times in their lives. Personal stance by its very nature is always transient.

The domains within personal stance are as follows shown in Figure 4.2.

Fragmentation
In this domain of personal stance, students experience challenges to their values and beliefs, which appear to be at risk or are threatened through this challenge and resultant uncertainty. Learning through problem-based learning may challenge students' current sense of self, and their way of both seeing the world and acting within it. This is because of the way in which problem-based learning encourages students to assemble their own body of knowledge and to make decisions about what counts as knowledge. Furthermore, being asked, through problem-based learning, to formulate their own decisions about what constitutes relevant learning results in students' prior experiences of learning, being a learner, understandings of knowledge and the role of the tutor, being challenged. This leads to a sense of fragmentation.

Figure 4.2　Domains within personal stance

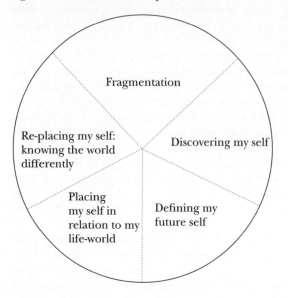

Discovering my self
In this domain, students' experiences of self-validation, which emerged in the context of the problem-based learning group, are the means by which self-discovery occurs. Self-discovery arises through forms of problem-based learning that promote a reflexive search for self-knowledge and self-improvement within students. Alternatively problem-based learning may prompt conflict, which forces a reappraisal of personal values and a re-evaluation of learner identity.

Defining my future self
In this domain students position themselves in the learning context in terms of their view of themselves as future professionals. They seek to understand themselves and the learning they are undertaking in terms of a perceived future role, and they see the material being learned in relation to their future self. The way students place themselves in the learning environment as a future professional governs the possibilities and limits of engagement with the material, the context and other people.

Placing my self in relation to my 'life-world'
In this domain students gain a heightened understanding of their own reality because of the way in which problem-based learning facilitates the mediation between their world and the world of higher and professional education and all that that entails. Learning in a problem-based way challenges students to confront the relationship between the previous experiences of their life-world (Habermas, 1989) and their new experiences emerging from

interaction with the objective world. This can lead to new understandings of their own reality. Thus, students might speak of inner resonance between their life-world and what they were learning.

Re-placing my self: knowing the world differently
The notion of 'knowing the world differently' captures the idea that students are able to frame their learning experiences for themselves and simultaneously challenge the institutions and sociopolitical contexts in which they live, work and learn. Students within this domain are able to take up alternative perspectives in order to challenge both themselves and the world. Thus within this domain the students value their own understanding and engage deeply with what is being learned, whilst simultaneously challenging both the validity of that understanding and also the material being learned.

Pedagogical stance

The notion of pedagogical stance was developed in order to encapsulate within the overarching framework of Dimensions of Learner Experience, the way in which students see themselves as learners. Students' pedagogical stances are constructed through a combination of their prior learning experiences, their often taken-for-granted notions of learning and teaching, and through the type of higher education that they receive. Higher education in the late 1990s and early 2000s is being encouraged to shift curricula in the direction of enabling students to develop pedagogical stances that are both flexible and market related. The institutional cultures in which students are learning appear to have a large bearing on the extent to which this shift is occurring.

Pedagogical stance depicts the way in which students see themselves as learners in particular educational environments. The choices students make within a learning situation and the particular learner history that they bring to a learning environment all influence students' pedagogical stance. Pedagogical stance may be affected by past success and failure. For example, surface approaches in learning, whereby the learner is more or less forced to adopt a rote-learning strategy (Marton and Säljö, 1976a, 1976b, 1984) or strategic approaches, characterized by the intention to maximize grades by strategic use of time and effort (Entwistle, 1987), may be adopted as the student sees this as the only means of ensuring a pass. Past failure may also result in students finding it difficult to attempt new and different ways of learning, which may involve personal risk. The concept of pedagogical stance acknowledges the relationship between the self and what is being learned.

Pedagogical stances also change in relation to other issues in people's lives, such as opting for a 'safer' way of learning when struggles elsewhere demand energy or resolution, or desiring greater challenge and change in learning when other aspects of life are mundane. Furthermore, the learner's self-perceived ability, and the conflicts or shared values that students have

Figure 4.3   Domains within pedagogical stance

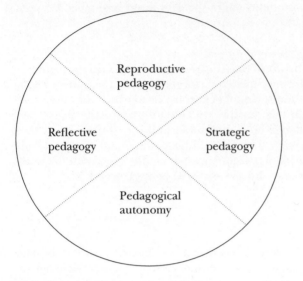

with tutors in those learning situations, may also affect the students' pedagogical stance.

The four domains within this stance are presented in Figure 4.3.

Reproductive pedagogy
Reproductive pedagogy encapsulates the idea that students may revert to methods of learning that they have always used, despite the considerable difference they may have encountered between methods of learning experienced at school compared with those at university. A tendency towards reproductive pedagogy may also occur because the nature of the curriculum reinforces surface approaches to learning. Alternatively reproductive pedagogy may be adopted by students who feel at risk in some way within the learning. Learning, for these students, is expected to be safe and predictable, requiring neither personal initiative nor critical thought. Teachers are seen to be the suppliers of all legitimate knowledge, since anything less will result in risk and failure for the students and inefficiency in their role as tutor. Students in this domain therefore tend to adopt methods of learning that maintain the *status quo* both for the student and in relation to the learning context.

Strategic pedagogy
Students in this domain may use several different learning strategies, but these are all within the remit of what is acceptable to both the authorities (institution, staff, profession) and the student. Here, pedagogical stance is characterized by a form of cue-seeking (Miller and Parlett, 1974) through

which students not only seek out cues in order to pass the assessment but also seek out cues from employers whilst on practice placements in order to discover which skills and knowledge will make them most employable. Students in this domain may adopt strategic approaches (Entwistle, 1981, 1987); however, the concept of strategic pedagogy extends the concept of strategic approaches by encompassing issues particular to higher education in the 1990s. For example, central issues include vocationalism and flexible career paths, whereby students are equipped to be adaptable to the changing demands of the world of work and to have a willingness to adapt to and to adopt, new values readily. Thus students in this domain see learning as being strategically linked to the world of work. Adapting their learning will ensure that they are equipped with the necessary skills and knowledge for the work place.

Pedagogical autonomy
Students here adopt a position of learning that they perceive will offer them the greatest degree of autonomy. They opt to learn in a way which suits them and that will offer them, as far as they are concerned, the most effective means of learning, meeting their own personally defined needs as learners yet also ensuring that they will pass the course. The nature of autonomy in this sense stems from the notion that learning for these students does not have to fit entirely within the remit of that defined by the authorities. What is important is that the means by which they learn is acceptable to themselves, and if what is on offer is not acceptable, it will be rejected in favour of something that is perceived to offer the desired autonomy. Thus the domain of pedagogical autonomy is characterized by the ability of students to be independent in making decisions about what and how they learn.

Reflective pedagogy
Reflective pedagogy encompasses the notion that students see learning and knowledge as flexible entities. Students within this domain perceive that there are valid perspectives other than their own, and they accept that all kinds of knowing can help them to 'know' the world better. This domain is characterized by critically evaluating personal knowledge and propositional knowledge on one's own terms; that is, the student both engages with knowledge yet also questions it. Thus, reflective pedagogy is a domain through which students see themselves and their learning as reflexive projects.

Interactional stance

Interactional stance is used here to capture the way in which a learner interacts with others within a learning situation. It refers to the relationships between students within groups, and staff–student relationships at both an individual and a group level. Interactional stance encompasses the way in which students interpret the way they as individuals, and others with whom they learn, construct meaning in relation to one another. The way in which one student may theorize about another student within a group setting reflects his interactional stance as does the way in which a student acts and speaks in interacting with other students. Interactional stance is also a notion that encompasses the means by which students engage with, and attribute meaning to, the processes that occur in groups. It is subsequently through reflection on these processes that students make sense of their own learning.

Groups are often talked about in terms of a journey, a progression where there are seen to be stages in which groups move from a forming stage through to a time of unity and effectiveness before they adjourn. In fact the problem-based learning groups were less stable, less convergent and less collaborative than the existing literature relating to groups and group theory implied. Students could point to unease connected both with their role within the group, the relationship between their individual concerns (that for some stood in direct conflict with the collective ethos of the group), and the nature of support within the group. It was unease that was cyclical rather than sequential in nature. Dilemmas were also verbalized. These predominantly related to staff's and students' concerns about particular issues that were felt might promote disabling experiences for students within the group, but that in many cases did in fact enhance learning. For example, the lack of resources at one site prompted in students an unexpectedly creative use of themselves as resources.

Conflict, which sprang from differing expectations and agenda about both the nature of learning within the group and the roles of group members and facilitators, emerged as a principal issue throughout the study. It was when describing conflicts within groups to which they belonged that students most often raised issues that could be said to reveal their interactional stance. For example, students spoke of conflict between the role expected of them by others within groups and their own perception and expectation of themselves as group members. Despite the unease, dilemmas and conflict experienced, the majority of students valued working in groups. Students' later reflections as practitioners demonstrated a deepening appreciation of both what they had gained through working in groups and of their under-standing of their own interactional stance.

Interactional stance comprises the domains shown in Figure 4.4.

The ethic of individualism

The 'ethic of individualism', after Lukes (1973), depicts the notion that some students see learning within the group as an activity that is only valuable in terms of what they as an individual could gain from it. These students place little value upon collective learning experiences and are more concerned that they may forgo marks by expending effort sharing tasks and information within the group rather than if they worked alone. This domain is characterized by the individual placing himself at the centre of the value system and therefore learning within the group is an activity that is only valuable in terms of personal gain for the individual.

Figure 4.4 Domains within interactional stance

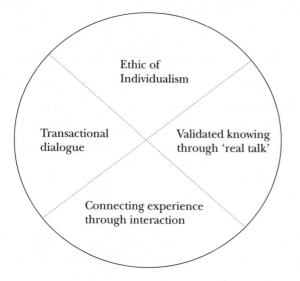

Validated knowing through 'real talk'
' "Really talking" requires careful listening; it implies a mutually shared agreement that together you are creating the optimum setting so that half-baked ideas can grow. "Real talk" reaches deep into the experience of each participant; it also draws on the analytical abilities of each' (Belenky *et al.*, 1986: 144). The domain of validated knowing captures the idea that through the experience of being heard within a group, and being valued by other group members, individual students learn to value their own knowledge and experience. Within a group where each member is valued and the optimum setting is created for ideas to grow, individuals feel empowered through affirmation. Prior experiences of the individual are valued as a resource for learning by other group members. Simultaneously prior experiences begin to be valued, sometimes for the first time, by the individuals, and subsequently are seen as a resource for further learning. For students in this domain learning in groups is often accompanied by a boost of self-esteem and confidence and, as a consequence, a renewed exploration and facilitation of individual learning aspirations. Being in this domain enables students to come to value their personal and propositional knowledge by recognizing its value through the perspectives of others.

Connecting experience through interaction
This domain is characterized by the individual being facilitated through the group process in making sense, through reflection, of his own reality and in confronting dilemmas and problems within that reality. For example, through role play or discussion within a group, students were enabled to make sense

of previous situations, experiences, or issues that they had not previously understood. Through interpretation of information about himself, and his experiences, obtained from other group members, the individual would learn to develop self-knowledge. Thus, in this domain students use the group to *make sense* of their world *as it appears to be* and will use the group to resolve dilemmas and discover meaning in their lives.

Transactional dialogue: mediating different worlds
Transactional dialogue (after Brookfield, 1985) is used here to capture the idea that the group serves as an interactive function for the individual. Through the group the individual is enabled to learn both through the experience of others and the appreciation of other people's life-worlds, and by reflecting upon these, to relate them to their own. Thus, individual students by making themselves and their learning the focus of reflection and analysis within the group, are able to value alternative ways of knowing. Dialogue here is central to progress in people's lives and it is through dialogue that values are deconstructed and reconstructed, and experiences relived and explored, in order to make sense of roles and relationships. This domain is concerned with identity building through the group process. For example, individuals within the transactional dialogue domain will use dialogue and argument as an organizing principle in life so that through dialogue they will challenge assumptions, make decisions and rethink goals. Students will use the group process to challenge identity and all that is implicit within that identity.

The framework of Dimensions of Learner Experience evolved through the subtleties of the struggles conveyed through the stories of participants. The stances, however, do overlap in a variety of ways and the interrelationship between them can be represented as shown in Figure 4.5.

Conclusion

The interrelationship between the stances can be seen through the manner in which students' pedagogical stances impacted upon their perceptions of themselves as group members, which in turn was often centred in their personal stance. For example, a student whose pedagogical stance was rooted in obtaining the best possible degree might take up an individualistic position in the group in order to support this pedagogical stance. Yet, this need to achieve high marks might be derived, at a level of subtext, from the student's personal stance. For example, an engineering student with a traditional view of education might define himself in such a way as to believe 'good engineers always get high marks'. This very intersection of personal and pedagogical stance could therefore have a disabling effect on the student's interactional stance, and consequently also the group of which that student was a member.

Figure 4.5   The stances and domains of Dimensions of Learner Experience

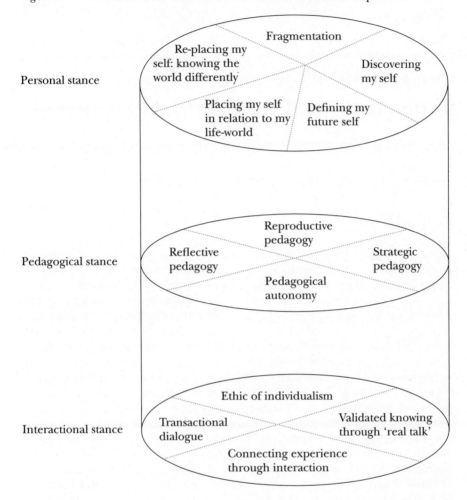

Students did not just 'have' a stance, it was something that they 'constructed' and which related to issues of identity, relationship with others and the learning context. Students, it seemed, related to problem-based learning through different dimensions of themselves and thus meaning was bound up with issues of learner identity and learner (prior) experience. Thus, Dimensions of Learner Experience in this study came to be used as a heuristic device to make sense of personal, pedagogical and interactional concerns within a framework. The next section presents the framework in the context of the lives, and stories, of students in order to demonstrate this complex interplay that exists when problem-based learning is in operation.

5

Images and Experiences of Problem-based Learning

Introduction

The framework of Dimensions of Learner Experience arose from analysis and interpretation of students' stories about their experiences of being involved in problem-based learning. It seems that problem-based learning offers a form of higher education that is more concerned with the aspirations and anxieties of the learner than that offered by the more didactic approaches to learning, because of the opportunities it provides for dialogue and the acknowledgement and integration of the self in the learning process. However, students also argued that problem-based learning prompted them to examine the relationship between their own conflicting experiences and their ideological images of learning. As such, problem-based learning prompted in many students an interrogation of themselves and their concepts of learning, and challenged them to engage in critical reflection. Such reflection, for some, was the beginning of a development towards a new way of understanding themselves. This chapter presents excerpts from students' accounts to demonstrate their images and experiences of learning, in the context of the framework of Dimensions of Learner Experience, as explained in Chapter 4.

Personal stance

Personal stance is used to depict the way in which participants see themselves in relation to the learning context and give their own distinctive meaning to their experience of that context. This chapter commences with an account of students' experiences and images in each of the five domains of personal stance.

Fragmentation

Students' experiences in this domain were characterized by a conflict between students' expectations of, and their encounter with, the learning context that contrasted sharply with prior learning experiences. This resulted in core aspects of their values and beliefs being threatened, which resulted in a sense of fragmentation. A number of students across the sites experienced poor self-esteem in the face of this threat and uncertainty. Others described what they felt was missing from their learning experience often by attributing blame, usually towards the tutor, for not being able to learn effectively through problem-based learning. What was missing also seemed to be connected with what they felt was missing from themselves, rather than necessarily from the learning experience. There were two key ways in which fragmentation occurred for students. First, students who did not feel able to take responsibility for their own learning blamed the tutors for this inability. Second, there were students who *were* able to learn for themselves through problem-based learning, yet who disliked and objected to the demands of this kind of independent enquiry, which brought with it a responsibility not required in previous experiences of learning.

The tendency to blame is illustrated by Sally who was a student undertaking nursing at Baslow. Sally's belief that her learning was someone else's responsibility stemmed from her uncompromising experiences in life: brought up in a religious family, Sally believed that there were clear guidelines and right answers. Her low self-esteem – she described herself as being 'not particularly intelligent' – had emerged from her position in the family as one of the few who had not achieved high grades at Advanced ('A') level whilst at school. This meant that she not only wanted to be told what to learn but also needed to be affirmed in the choices she had made:

> You need to know, are you doing the right thing? Are you doing the wrong thing? You don't know if you've never come across it before what is right and what is wrong, do you? What is the right way to go about something and what is the wrong way? And you might be doing it all wrong but because nobody's said any different to you, you go through with the feeling you're doing it right.

Sally expected not only that the tutors would provide her with the knowledge and skills that she needed to become a nurse, but that they would also show her how to make connections between herself and what she was learning. As a student nurse undergoing clinical practice she received clear instructions about the right way to undertake tasks, in lectures she was given a body of knowledge, but during problem-based learning days she was expected to take responsibility for her own learning. Sally experienced fragmentation because of the way in which the assumptions implicit in learning through problem-based learning jarred with her own assumptions about learning. This was in terms of both her prior learning experiences and learning which had occurred in other areas of the curriculum that were not problem-based. Thus, her sense of fragmentation stemmed not only from internal conflict but also through the contradictions between differing understandings of the learning that she experienced at Baslow.

Discovering my self

A number of students spoke of the way in which problem-based learning had offered them a learning situation in which they had felt able to promote their own development and self-discovery. A number of students spoke about self-validation as a positive experience, which occurred through support from others, often peers, sometimes staff, periodically both. The existence and nature of support available, from staff or peers, appeared to be key to the extent to which self-discovery was experienced as positive or negative.

Jack's perspective demonstrates the way in which a number of students experienced support, and subsequently self-validation, through questioning. Jack, at Lembert, had been an apprentice for four years after leaving school at 16. He did an Ordinary National Certificate (ONC) in mechanical engineering and worked his way up from fitter to manager. He chose to undertake the AMD engineering course because his hobby was tinkering with cars, and he wanted to integrate his interest with skill and knowledge of engineering. Jack's previous encounter with learning on a didactic ONC course had silenced him into thinking that his prior experience was not of value, but after engaging with problem-based learning he felt that the learning on the ONC course had been meaningless in comparison. Jack reflected on how his view of learning had changed through being able to question:

> One of the other things we've been taught to do is never be frightened to ask a question, no matter how stupid it is. That's one of the things they always keep saying to us 'Just ask, don't be worried about making a fool of yourself.' Because so often people just sit there and pretend they understand because they feel they ought to and then afterwards try and find out whereas in this course we are encouraged more to ask no matter how stupid the questions are . . . but of course when you're in industry you spend all your time asking people so you've got to learn, you know, you've got everything to learn. So this sort of teaches you to do that, to ask.

Jack's view reflected the essence of the way in which many students discovered that learning was not just about receiving information, it was about taking responsibility for their own learning in a way that was unique to each individual. Jack now saw learning as a means of understanding both himself, and content and process, in relation to the world around him. Being encouraged to question appeared to promote in students self-validation, which fostered self-development.

Defining my future self

Some students described themselves in terms of their perceived future role, and others in terms of the relationship between their current self and perceived future self. Several students classified their personal stance in terms of 'being a good engineer', 'thinking like a designer' and 'more of a student than a nurse'. Many defined themselves in relation to qualities either to which they aspired or with which they did not wish to be associated. For example, Janet, who, having experienced failure in her General Certificates of Secondary Education (GCSE), attended a sixth-form college to retake the examinations and to subsequently sit 'A' levels, was used to making decisions about what and how she learned. Sixth-form college had enabled her to develop an autonomy not possible at school, but at Baslow she encountered attitudes and values, both on campus and in practice, which mimicked her school days and which she saw as barriers to autonomy. She believed that as a student training to be a nurse she was caught between two roles. As a student nurse at university the clinical practice component and the extra weeks that she was required to undertake to fulfil the hours prescribed by the professional body meant that she did not fit into the normal student pattern of semesters and vacations. Furthermore, doing shift work during clinical practice placements meant she was unable to attend university activities. As a nurse she was not undertaking the traditional unquestioning apprenticeship model of learning, and was required to return to university one day a week during clinical practice weeks to question and reflect on practice.

The freedom in the problem-based learning days offered Janet the auto-nomy and challenge she had enjoyed at sixth-form college, and this was the catalyst that prompted her to define herself as a student rather than a nurse. For Janet being a student encapsulated the notion of autonomy (freedom to think and to learn independently) and exploration. This con-trasted sharply with the expected obedience and conformity to professional norms that she experienced on placement, despite the fact that apart from the oasis of autonomy in the problem-based learning days, the course was didactic and tightly structured. Unlike the women, the men in this domain tended to be clear about their role as future professionals, and problem-based learning had been a means of enhancing their understanding of these roles. Bill at Lembert, for example, defined himself as 'being an engineer'. He spoke of his personal stance in terms of a making sense, of an under-standing that emerged out of a personal interest in the subject. Bill was a school leaver who had wanted to go to a university with more kudos than Lembert, but who did not achieve the 'A' level grades required. Five ring-binder files full of information, which he neither remembered nor under-stood, symbolized his first year of dissonance on the mechanical engineering degree programme, which he was obliged to undertake before the more appealing applied AMD engineering course. Yet, through the problem-based learning programme an inner resonance with the material being learned emerged from his perception that it directly related to his future professional life. This stood in marked contrast to his feelings of estrangement from the first year lecture material, which he felt to be irrelevant to his future career.

Placing my self in relation to my life-world

For the majority of the students, it was this domain of personal stance through which problem-based learning had enabled them to both discover and give meaning to their 'life-world'. Students here spoke of being able, often for the first time, to engage effectively with what was being learned, through a heightened awareness of the relationship between their prior experience and the material.

Valuing and acknowledging prior experience is seen by many to be a key component of problem-based learning (Barrows and Tamblyn, 1980; Boud and Feletti, 1997) and this was captured by Olive who spoke of her personal stance in terms of personal empowerment, which occurred through a change in perspective. Olive described herself as having no academic background and, being reluctant to undertake a course with examinations, the diploma in social work at Stanage had appealed to her. She had been working as a volunteer for the Probation Service and this prompted her to train as a probation officer. Reflecting on her role as a parent was something through which Olive was challenged:

> Because I've got three kids, it's actually brought up quite a lot of stuff about socializing children and what is right, you know, what you should do as a parent, especially doing the child protection and now we're doing adolescence. And it's actually been more reassuring rather than threatening. Part of it has been a review of how I did, and having a look at my own practice of child rearing, which has brought up quite a lot of painful stuff, but it's also been quite reassuring as well . . . Part of it is about getting rid of stuff and moving on, and it's about acquiring skills as well. I am in the process of acquiring skills, I'm not there. And an awareness that there are things I do want to be acquired.

Through problem-based learning Olive had developed a new understanding of her own reality and had begun to shift towards understanding the way in which other worlds beside her own had been damaged by political systems, government policy and social issues such as poverty and lack of education. So apart from reviewing her own history, she also saw the need to review that of others with whom she would be working in the future. Placing herself was not just about engaging with what was being learned and making sense of it in the context of her own life and the world in which she had chosen to work, it was also about seeing the world in a different way and learning for social change.

Re-placing my self: knowing the world differently

Several students had begun to move *towards* the position of 'knowing the world differently' in the sense that they had begun to move in the direction of taking a stance towards re-evaluating their current views and perspectives. Yet Ian, undertaking a social work diploma, had in fact made a shift to knowing the world differently. His notion of personal stance captured the ideal that through valuing his own understanding of himself, his life-world, his learning and the learning context, and the objective world, it was simultaneously possible to challenge the validity of this understanding. Ian saw his personal stance, although he did not speak directly in these terms, as his self in transition: he spoke of his relationship with what was being learned as a cyclical process in which he continually honed his values in relation to new material he was encountering. For example, he saw learning situations as being open-ended so that new material (whether it was knowledge, skills or values) which he encountered in learning was not necessarily expected to supersede the old. Instead, all, some or none of it was integrated. Thus, existing values and ideals may or may not be replaced or displaced by new ones. Although he acknowledged that problem-based learning had facilitated – through reading or discussion with other students – an exploration of his current values, he argued that problem-based learning did not always prompt students to consider the relationship between their own personal philosophies and those of social work. He explained:

> Issues like child protection (is a key issue for me) because it's forced people to confront their own particular perspectives and the way they act in social work – I mean, there are other things as well like homelessness and the myths about homelessness and that gave me a chance personally to provide that different perspective within the structure at the time. So it's a lot of times provided a chance for people to understand that people do have slightly different approaches to issues, and that sometimes that's a good thing, and that making decisions in a social work situation you are in effect looking at it from your own perspective and your own philosophy, which is very strong in community work, but I don't think it's that strong in social work.

Ian's view was that individuals should be aware of their own political agenda and personal prejudice and bias, and that they should therefore be clear about what they were bringing to a situation when dealing with clients. Through problem-based learning Ian had been both prompted and enabled to confront the issues that underpinned his own practice and to challenge them. His personal stance was characterized by a process of continual reflexivity – a more or less continuous interrogation of past, present and future – by making himself the subject of his own analysis so that as an individual he was in a constant stage of transition.

Pedagogical stance

Pedagogical stance encapsulates the way in which learners see themselves as learners. Students' pedagogical stances are constructed through a combination of their prior learning experiences, their often taken-for-granted notions of learning and teaching, and through the type of higher education that they receive. The four domains of pedagogical stance are as follows:

Reproductive pedagogy

In reproductive pedagogy students choose to use methods of learning with which they feel familiar and which pose little challenge to their identity as learners, or their understandings of their life-world.

Phil, a student at Gimmer, ensured that his marks were as high as possible by taking control in the group. It was he who collated and edited the group's written reports, and who took a lead in the group presentations. Phil's stance was thus characterized by being offered, and adopting, an opportunity to learn in ways which were, for him, both familiar and effective. He had obtained high grades in 'A' level science and had been obliged to opt for the problem-based learning module in vibration engineering as his final year project was also in this subject. Throughout his degree he had chosen exam-based modules in order to 'get the best marks' and believed that any sense of enjoying and connecting personally with what was being learned was secondary to obtaining a good degree. Phil defined himself as someone who was competent in passing examinations. Through a knowledge of himself and his capacity as a 'skilled student', he distinguished studying from learning which might entail personal engagement, in order to read the system and make it work for him. Thus, his pedagogical stance was characterized by assimilating and reproducing information supplied by academics, on academics' terms.

For a number of students across the sites there was a sense of being driven into reproductive pedagogy through forms of disjunction prompted by issues which appeared to be beyond their control. Disjunction that was disabling in nature seemed to arise either through conflicts between staff's espoused theories and their theories-in-use, or from the relationship between prior learning experiences and new and different ones. For these students disabling disjunction experienced within this domain appeared to be a transitional phase *en route* to other domains. For example, students who felt trapped in reproductive pedagogy through hidden agenda imposed by staff were later able to transcend staff's agenda in preference for their own. This occurred through forms of disjunction that were, or became, enabling and resulted in a greater sense of integration.

Strategic pedagogy

A third of the students adopted strategic pedagogy, choosing to embrace the perceptions of staff expectations of learning, in anticipation that it would be the most effective means of passing the course. The migration into the academic world of strategic values that focus more on achieving some externally validated end, rather than the validation of interactive and collaborative forms of learning and reasoning, is resulting in students focusing more on strategy and less on the values of process. Strategic values focus on achievement and outcomes, and on innovation for profitability and survival. Thus, in this sense higher education today seems to promote pragmatic responses to problems in society, whilst downgrading the kinds of reasoning that encourage students to form their own ideas and judgements and to keep their own critical distance from all they experience within a course. Students within this domain adopted strategic forms of reasoning rather than taking up an approach to learning that focused on process and outcome in a critical way. Emily's experience illustrates this issue.

Emily had left school and taken 'A' levels at technical college before coming to Baslow. Although Emily thought the nursing course was 'quite strict' she valued the freedom in learning that she experienced in the problem-based learning days. Yet she was uncomfortable about the conflict she experienced on the ward as a result of the preparation work for the problem-based learning days. Students were given a worksheet at the end of the problem-based learning day and were required to choose a topic that they would subsequently research during the following week on the wards. Carrying out this research caused conflict for both the nurse practitioners and the students. Emily explained:

> We had these worksheets that we had to do ... but most of the time I was working just as hard as everybody else was on the ward even though I was just a student. I didn't really want to sit down and look as if all I was doing was taking notes, I just wanted to get on with it really. Particularly as we're known as the Uni nurses that do nothing practical really. They're not particularly keen on degree nurses, particularly in Baslow General I don't think, and a lot of them are quite stand-offish at first. And I think if we sat down at the nursing desk and basically filled out our little forms and our project books and everything like that I think that really didn't help our situation at all. I think it was just better for us to get in and start learning from other people rather than filling in questionnaires.

Although Emily valued the opportunity for self-direction and independent study encouraged by problem-based learning, because it enabled her to integrate theory with practice, she opted for strategic pedagogy to ensure she passed her placement. At Baslow many nurse practitioners were socializing students into the apprenticeship model of learning where student nurses were not expected to think and reflect, but to do as they were told. Thus, students were encouraged to work within frameworks that directed their decision making within practice, and adopt forms of knowledge entirely related to these frameworks.

Pedagogical autonomy

Students in this domain adopt a position of learning that they perceive will offer them the greatest degree of autonomy. Students positioned within this domain demonstrated an ability to be, or to become, independent in making decisions about what and how they learned. The degree of autonomy possible within each problem-based learning programme was not only affected by learner history and self-esteem, but also by staff-espoused theories and theories-in-use, through the type of guidance on offer and by the degree of responsibility students were both able, and encouraged to take, for their own learning.

Alice at Stanage was one of a number of students who raised the notion of being 'deskilled'. Being 'deskilled' captured a theme about students experiencing learning as something that was different from their previous understanding of it, resulting in a feeling of being ill-equipped to cope with a new way of learning. It also reflected something about feeling at odds with themselves in terms of not being sure how to integrate their current roles and experiences with those of their past and future.

During her sociology degree Alice had attended lectures and had largely worked independently. Working and learning in a problem-based learning group had challenged her notion of learning and also the values that she had placed on learning on her own. Thus, for Alice conflict was caused by experiencing two contrasting methods of learning that had different values and emphases. For example, working on her own and attending lectures conflicted with the ethos of problem-based learning at Stanage with its emphasis on collaborative learning. As a result she experienced conflict in learning how to learn through problem-based learning and learning about her role as a group member. Yet this conflict brought about enabling disjunction through which Alice was able to understand what it was she valued in a learning experience. This occurred in two ways. First, she was prompted through problem-based learning to explore her own understanding of what constituted learning. Second, the self-validation she experienced through the groups to which she belonged enabled her to assess critically her prior experience and roles, and to realize that in fact she had not actually been deskilled, but reaffirmed in her skills and abilities.

Reflective pedagogy

Within this domain students accept that all kinds of knowing can help them to 'know' the world better. Learning involves evaluating critically not only the knowledge supplied by academics and professionals, but also the values implicit within that knowledge.

Clare was one student who experienced disjunction that was enabling within her personal stance, which subsequently facilitated transition in her pedagogical stance. Clare's expectation of, and initial encounter with, the learning experience had primarily resulted in disjunction that challenged her perception of knowledge. The fragmentation in her personal stance meant that she saw herself as a learner who had acquired disparate chunks of knowledge, which would eventually cohere, and thus within her pedagogical stance she focused on the gaps between the chunks of knowledge. Disjunction in her pedagogical stance resulted from her expectations that staff would enable her to fill these gaps. She found that staff did not see themselves as gap fillers and realized that it was no longer 'the sort of phenomenon of tutors as experts and us there, just sort of receiving pearls of wisdom', but that she was expected both to make her own knowledge, and to make knowledge her own. Disjunction within her pedagogical stance resulted in transition. Clare moved from reproductive pedagogy where she saw learning as the acquisition of facts supplied by academics – as experienced during her first degree – to reflective pedagogy where learning involved not only critically evaluating knowledge but also the values implicit within that knowledge. Clare reflected upon her learning experiences:

> Its not just sort of helping you to get to grips with child protection procedure and stuff like that, its more issue based . . . I think the point of view of gaining awareness and insight is also a valuable approach. I think awareness and insight of ourselves and our needs, its very important in social work that you have that self-awareness, that you're aware of your needs, you're aware of your own values and perceptions and reactions and so on, as a worker going out into the field.

Whereas for Jackie, another social work student at Stanage, her personal and pedagogical stances were inextricably linked. She argued that she found it difficult to 'talk about problem-based learning in the course separately from me as a person and my kind of life pattern and processes'. Jackie's view of herself as someone who was academically capable, and who was confident in her own ability to question the knowledge and ethical principles laid before her, meant that she was prepared to take risks and challenge the status quo. Jackie saw knowledge as something that was to be challenged and explored not only within the framework of the university but also within practice, and across the culture of both practice and higher education.

Interactional stance

Interactional stance captures the way in which a learner interacts with others within a learning situation. It refers to the relationships between students within groups, and staff–student relationships at both an individual, and a group level. Thus, interactional stance encompasses the way in which students interpret the way they as individuals, and others with whom they learn, construct meaning in relation to one another. The four domains of interactional stance in the context of students' experiences are presented below:

The ethic of individualism

Students within this domain saw the value of working and learning within groups because they recognized that they would need skills in teamwork for their future profession. Despite this they opted for isolation and individualism because they saw this approach as enabling them to obtain a better qualification.

Chris, at Gimmer, was a student who valued the opportunity to work and learn in a group. He valued the opinions of his peers and also the opportunity to discuss different ideas about the problem situation that they were attempting to manage. However, towards the end of the problem-based learning module he began to wonder about the value of problem-based learning to him as an individual. He resented the losses of his own time and own opinion that he experienced through committing himself to the group. For example, Chris had been made to wait for several hours while different group members arrived late for the meeting and left early. Furthermore, he felt his own opinion had been lost amidst the need to reach a group decision, 'I feel that we've got four leaders, four chiefs and no Indians. I feel we're compromising ourselves just to get something together as a group. I'm not sure that's the best way of getting things done.' Chris had originally valued problem-based learning, and found that learning in a group had initially enabled him to feel valued as a group member and empowered through that affirmation. However, he experienced disabling disjunction through other group members putting their own needs before that of the group, which had resulted in Chris adopting a similar approach. Thus, the collective ethos of learning was destroyed by students choosing to work for their own ends rather than for those of the group.

Validated knowing through 'real talk'

Much of the real learning that occurred through problem-based learning in this study arose through group interaction but this was seldom rewarded in academic terms. Validated knowing captures the idea that through the experience of being heard within a group, and being valued by other group members, individual students learn to value their own knowledge and experience. Students spoke of 'making sense', 'connecting', 'seeing things in a new way', all within the context of the group. Thus, for many students learning that occurred in relation to the group process actually held more meaning than learning which was rewarded through assessment.

Two women from Stanage capture the essence of the issues within this domain. They spoke specifically about the way in which they felt endorsed and valued as individuals through the experience of learning within groups. Their differing interactional stances, occurring in the same domain, were spoken of in terms of learning that occurred only with, and in relation to, others; and it was through this that they had experienced self-validation.

Nicola and Alice came to value their prior experiences through the experience of being valued by other members of the group to which they belonged. Nicola had discovered that in one component of the course she was one of the experts in her group on children's work. Being an expert helped her to develop confidence and realize the value of her prior experiences, but also enabled her to develop a more active role in the group than the role she had previously taken. Alice had had her own perspectives challenged within the group but simultaneously had experienced validation of her prior experience:

> With this course you realize skills that you've got and you can find out ways of developing those skills and knowledge and sharing it with the group. It's like brilliant when you know something and just sharing it with the group . . . things like, counselling skills, listening skills, skills about how you go about looking at particular issues or dilemmas and just like thinking about how you'd go about doing things really . . . I can see I've learnt quite a lot since I've been on this course. And I think you get a lot of that from the group situation, having the situation where people are acknowledging people's skills in the group.

Self-validation had enabled Alice not only to realize the virtues of problem-based learning but also to assemble discrete skills and knowledge, so that she was able to both draw on and develop her own abilities.

Connecting experience through interaction

A number of students spoke of the way in which learning and reflection within groups had enabled them to make sense of their own experience as learners.

Two themes emerged about the way in which students were enabled to connect their experience through interaction within the group. First, students across the sites used groups to enable themselves to make sense of the interrelationship of their problem-solving processes, prior experience and the new material being learned. Luke at Lembert demonstrated the essence of the experience of several students in terms of the way in which he was enabled to make sense of reality through discussion in problem-based learning groups.

Luke argued that the group to which he belonged had gone through a process of transformation since its inception two terms ago, and he felt he had grown and developed through that process. For example, when the group first began to tackle the given problems they expected the solutions to be straightforward answers similar to those that would result from the tutorial sheet of a lecture-based component of the course which had one basic answer. It was through dialogue that Luke had learned that the process of problem-solving in problem-based learning was more complex and that he could utilize group members to explore different ways of tackling the problem. Luke explained this process:

> I think when you first get the problem, I think that's when the group works best because out of the four of you there's bound to be someone where a bit of its clicked and he explains it in normal English and then the others say 'oh yeah, yeah and I suppose this means that' and the ball really starts to get rolling.

'Explaining it in normal English' was the process through which the students were enabled to interpret what appeared to be an objective situation and together transform it into something that made sense in relation to their individual and collective life-world(s). On each occasion when the group worked through a process of problem-solving it promoted group cohesion, mutual understanding and personal development.

Second, students used the groups to explore their personal stance. For example, several students at Stanage tended to utilize groups according to their perceived needs as future professionals, and as places in which they could explore different ways of operating within groups in preparation for working as practitioners. Other students, across the sites, tended to use groups to enable themselves to make sense of issues that arose on practice placements.

Transactional dialogue: mediating different worlds

In this domain the group serves as an interactive function for the individual. Here dialogue is central to progress in people's lives, since through it values are deconstructed and reconstructed, and experiences relived and explored, in order to make sense of roles and relationships.

For Douglas at Lembert learning to work in a group was not just about learning how to learn in a group environment, but also learning about democracy, loyalty and effective team work. He learned that his focus had to be the achievement of the task with a spirit of cooperation, rather than putting his and other people's individuality before the achievement of the task. Although in terms of the course he realized that the aim was to solve the given problem, he saw learning in groups in the broader context as offering opportunities to understand and explore other people's perspectives. Douglas talked about this in terms of 'learning to exist with people' and 'choosing to get on with them'. For him learning with and through others was something that required effort and had to be worked at, and it was only through this that he could hope to understand other people's perspectives (and life-worlds). Dialogue offered Douglas the opportunity to explore differing ways of knowing, which would ultimately offer him an increased understanding of the way in which roles and relationships affected his effectiveness as an engineer.

For Olive, undertaking social work training, it was through reflecting on her experiences of other people's perspectives within the group that empowered her to adopt different reasoning strategies than those she had previously used, in order to deal with unfamiliar situations. Through reflecting on both the experience of peers, and the way in which she had integrated the theory of that experience and knowledge into her own life-world, she was able to confront and make sense of dilemmas in practice. Olive found that problem scenarios she had encountered on campus and explored within the context of the group had equipped her to deal with similar issues on placement. Olive's background of working in the probation service had furnished her with a wide variety of experience, but little in the realm of working with families. She explained the way in which working through problems in the context of the group had helped her to supply practical advice to a client. This advice was based on strategies and guidance she had gained through the group:

> I went on placement, working with families, because I've never done that before. I've worked with offenders and gone into their homes and talked to their wives and seen the children and everything else. But what I'd be looking for, what I'd be thinking about was totally focused in a different way... because some of the scenarios that I actually had coming through the door, *[on placement]* I actually dealt with, I'd actually done, I'd actually done somebody who'd been beaten up by their husband and what you would do. And I found that incredibly helpful, you know. And I actually had some of the, not answers, but suggestions about where she should go from there. And that was helpful. I had good practical stuff and that came straight from a study group, not from a facilitator but from people who've worked in that field.

She had been enabled through the group to adapt her public role as she encountered for herself a reality experienced by others. It was through dialogue within the group that she was able to relate to the life-world of a client through a mediation between her life-world, the life-worlds of peers and the external world. Thus, for Douglas and Olive transactional dialogue was encapsulated in the process of learning to engage with the life-worlds of others and through reflection, to relate other life-worlds to their own. It was through this relatedness that they were able to challenge assumptions, make decisions and adopt new strategies and ways of knowing.

The interrelationship between the stances

The interface between stances were captured poignantly through the individual stories of students and one story in particular will be presented here to illustrate the effect of the stances on each other in the context of students' lives.

After leaving school at 16, Jack had been an apprentice for four years before undertaking an ONC in mechanical engineering. When I first met Jack his story was characterized by enthusiasm for problem-based learning and appreciation of the way in which learning this way had enabled him to find meaning in the material he was expected to learn. Jack's prior learning experiences had led him to assume that learning comprised rote memorization of facts, which he felt bore little relationship to both his own interests and the world of work. The difficulties Jack experienced in learning through didactic methods resulted in a belief that it was necessarily he who was unsatisfactory, rather than the system. His experience of problem-based learning challenged Jack to revisit his perceptions about his own learning, which resulted in an overall sense of disjunction.

Personal stance: from discovering my self to defining my future self

Enabling disjunction, which Jack experienced within his personal stance, initially resulted in a shift towards learning that held real meaning for him. As he progressed through the course he became increasingly integrated in this domain, which prompted a shift into 'defining my future self'. Jack thus began to position himself in the learning context in terms of his view of himself as a future professional. He sought to understand himself and the learning he was undertaking in terms of a perceived future role. Yet it was not only support from staff that produced this transition, it was enabling and disabling disjunction within other stances. For example, support from peers and heightened self-esteem gained through the group enabled him to reevaluate his learning goals. Within strategic pedagogy his dissatisfaction with some staff's notion of problem-based learning challenged him to adopt strategic methods which would enhance his chances of gaining a good degree.

Pedagogical stance: away from a sense of integration within strategic pedagogy

Jack experienced disabling disjunction within this domain. First, he found that even by buying into the academics' notion of problem-based learning he was not always enabled to develop himself and explore areas that he valued. Application and understanding were issues that Jack felt were key to being able to apply his knowledge. They were skills that had enabled him to learn to resolve or manage problem situations effectively by using his knowledge in a way in which he had been unable to do on the mechanical engineering course in the first year. However, now, in the fourth year, he felt angry when some tutors imposed their own strategies on the students. He believed he had not been offered the opportunities to develop his problem-solving capacity fully. He objected to these artificial discipline boundaries, and the ways in which he had been prevented from exploring various aspects of the given problem due to the inculcation of a step-by-step approach to problem-solving by some of the staff.

Interactional stance: away from a sense of integration within validated knowing through 'real talk'

Paradoxically the sense of enabling disjunction through which Jack had gained confidence through 'real talk' within the group was also the means by which he later experienced disabling disjunction within this stance. Experiencing enabling disjunction had caused him to review and reflect upon his individual learning aspirations both within and beyond the group. Yet conflict, which sprang from differing expectations and agenda about both the nature of learning within the group and the roles of group members, emerged as a key issue for Jack. Rather than try to continue to facilitate an effective group process he chose to work less assiduously on behalf of the group and focus more on his own aspirations. It was the heightened self-esteem gained through the group that gave Jack the confidence to implement this transition. Despite this he saw it as a negative and disabling step both for himself and the group, particularly because he believed learning with and through the group was still more effective than opting for a more individualistic position.

Thus, it has been possible to see that personal, pedagogical and interactional stances are necessarily interlinked and affect one another since together they offer a multifaceted view of learner experience. The influence of the stances on each student varied according to particular students and their circumstances. For example, the learning context and the ways in which students saw themselves in relation to that context affected the pedagogical stances they felt were on offer or that they believed they could take up. Thus, different students adopted different strategies for managing learning, which connected with their perceived notions of staff's view of knowledge. These differences related to the kinds of knowledge that were allowed to be examined and the ways in which students were expected to explore this knowledge by staff and practitioners. Students' and staff's pedagogical stances also affected students' interactional stances because of the requirement for students, through the group, to meet staff's pedagogical agenda. For example, students spoke specifically about the way in which they had used the groups to reflect on the information with which they had been presented. They also used the group to explore and make sense of personal challenges that emerged from the interrelationship between their personal and pedagogical stance. This, for many students, resulted in a realization that they had in fact understood more about lecture material and problem scenarios than they had initially realized. Students' ability to 'connect through interaction' in their interactional stance therefore enhanced their ability to make decisions regarding the domain they adopted in their pedagogical stance and challenged them to (re)consider the domain they had taken up in their personal stance.

Conclusion

This framework highlights the paradox that the study, which began as a quest to make sense of problem-based learning became instead an enquiry, an argument and indeed a (self-reflective) dialogue about how learners construct their experience. Students' stories of problem-based learning could not be separated from the ways in which they talked about themselves, their learner identity and the learning context. What also seemed to be important was that disjunction, whether enabling or disabling in nature, seemed to be central not only to learner experience but also in changes connected with learner identity. The concept of disjunction and the challenges it raises for staff and students is explored next, in Chapter 6.

Part 3

Learning at the Borders

6

Recognizing Disjunction

Introduction

This chapter explores the concept of disjunction in learning. It begins by documenting ways in which disjunction occurs in the context of students' lives and then moves on to consider the kinds of catalyst to disjunction that emerge when problem-based learning is in operation. To recap: disjunction is used here to refer to a sense of fragmentation of part of, or all of the self, characterized by frustration and confusion, and a loss of sense of self. This often results in anger, frustration, and a desire for 'right' answers.

It is noticeable that disjunction is an area addressed by few in the field of problem-based learning and in higher education in general. However, given the nature of disjunction and the way in which it affects learning and learner experience, there needs to be some exploration not only of it as a concept but also of the ways in which it is managed (and mismanaged). There is also a need to explore where the responsibility lies in enabling the process of effective management of disjunction to occur. I argue that disjunction is not something to be seen as unhelpful and damaging, but instead as dynamic in the sense that different forms of disjunction: enabling and disabling, can result in transitions in students' lives. Such transitions can help students to re-examine and challenge their personal and professional framework. The chapter concludes with an examination of the ways in which particular types of circumstances give rise to disjunction and suggests four different approaches that students may adopt to deal with disjunction.

Disjunction: a barrier to learning?

Across different learning environments it is possible to see that students often encounter barriers to learning whether they are undergraduate school leavers, research students or those attending adult education classes. Yet it seems there is little to guide educators or students to enable them to recognize these barriers to learning and the often resulting sudden arrest in the progress of learning. For many students obstacles in learning are experienced as issues that are seldom expected. The very nature of disjunction means that managing it presents a challenge to the individual, which in turn may result in disjunction being seen as something negative, undesirable and as a barrier rather than a gateway to learning. Yet these barriers *do* exist and there seems to be little to offer students who encounter them. Students not only have to learn to manage disjunction for themselves but also that a failure to manage it successfully is likely to mean that the issue(s) which was the initial catalyst to disjunction will continue to inhibit their progress until it is managed effectively. Jarvis (1987) has argued that disjunction lies at the heart of learning and that the closer it is to the person's system of meaning, the greater the imperative to respond to it. He has also suggested that all learning begins with experience and that it is the environment within which the experience is provided which helps to determine the type of learning that ensues, since it is the meaning which the learner places upon situations that affects the learning process thereafter.

Shifts away from disjunction always seem to be related to students experiencing a greater sense of integration. Although for many, integration is characterized by the whole self being in equilibrium, more often it is described as a particular component of the self being in balance. Thus, integration can be experienced in very distinct ways by different people at different times in their lives. Shifts away from integration tend to result in an individual being in a position where their previous way of seeing and knowing the world holds less or little meaning in their current situation.

Disjunction as a pedagogical concern?

Since disjunction is a common occurrence for students in different educational environments, it is important to explore catalysts to disjunction so that effective strategies for managing the experience can be developed. As disjunction is not something readily understood it is therefore not easily managed, particularly as it does not tend to occur as a result of a simplistic cause and effect relationship. Instead it is multifaceted in nature and 'emerges out of mutually interacting influences' (Weil, 1989: 112). Staff who set up modes of learning such as group work or problem-based learning that may cause a distinct challenge to students' life-worlds, will need to treat disjunction, and its management, as a pedagogical concern.

Yet disjunction does not only occur in relation to learning that is seen by students to be relevant and meaningful. Disjunction also occurs because students experience challenges to their life-world, challenges which are at odds with, or bear little relationship to, their current meaning systems. Dewey argued that the central problem of an education based on experience is in the selection of experiences that will ultimately be fruitful. If, therefore, disjunction is an experience that is consistently mismanaged and consequently disabling in nature, then learning experiences which prompt disjunction are likely to be miseducative. Dewey argued that:

> Experience and education cannot be directly equated with each other. For some experiences are miseducative. Any experience is miseducative that has the effect of arresting or distorting the growth of further experience. An experience may be such as to engender callousness; it may produce lack of sensitivity and of responsiveness. Then the possibilities of having richer experience in the future are restricted.
>
> (Dewey, 1938: 13)

Students who experience disjunction which is disabling will often find ways of managing it through the dialogue and opportunities for making sense of it that stem from working and learning in problem-based groups. These experiences will help them to avoid the callousness of which Dewey spoke. For many students, discovering meaning also occurs through groups because of the ways in which they connect with, and find meaning in, the life-worlds of others, and then make a shift themselves towards a greater sense of integration. Thus, disjunction may be educative or miseducative but also enabling or disabling. Furthermore students can experience disjunction, which can be enabling in one stance whilst being disabling in another. For example, a student may experience fragmentation within his personal stance because of the disjunction he encounters in attempting to manage multiple and conflicting roles in the context of a practice placement. Such disjunction can be enabling because of the way in which it enables him, despite the sense of fragmentation, to see that he is managing the uncertainty connected with role conflicts. At the same time the student may be trapped in reproductive pedagogy in his pedagogical stance because of the way in which practice placement staff's expectations about student learning, and what it means to be a learner, stand in direct contrast to his own expectations of learning. This disjunction is initially disabling, but may later become enabling if, for example, students and staff examine and explore their own conceptions of learning. Yet it does not follow necessarily that forms of disjunction which are disabling are always miseducative, since disjunction which is disabling can lead to enabling forms of learning, through prompting students to challenge and transcend boundaries which had previously been barriers to growth and development. However, there are key issues that seem to prompt different kinds of disjunction for students, in diverse ways. These may be seen as a series of catalysts.

Catalysts to disjunction

Catalysts to disjunction become apparent through staff and students' increasing awareness of an interplay of multiple realities, roles and identities, which seem to arise when problem-based learning is in operation. In learning contexts there exist distinct contradictions for different individuals, groups of people and organizations, which may prompt disjunction for individuals in different ways. For example, issues that at first appear enabling for a number of students, such as the opportunity for self-direction, can in fact be disabling for others. Alternatively, the implementation of problem-based learning by a particular group of staff within an institution can, at one level, be seen as something that will promote reasoning skills and prepare students more effectively for the world of work; whereas in practice the implementation of problem-based learning can result in conflict for a number of staff, students and practitioners about what is seen to count as knowledge and how notions of accountability are to be understood within professional education.

New and different learning experiences

Disjunction occurs for many individuals because they do not know how to manage new and different ways of learning. For example, many of those students who believe, on joining the course, that they understand what constitutes problem-based learning may not realize the challenges and conflicts which may ensue. For most, prior experiences will be of traditional, didactic methods of teaching that offered little opportunity for them to value their own knowledge and perspectives. However, over a period of time students may learn to use problem-based learning groups to make sense of the interrelationship between their problem-solving processes, prior experience and the new material being learned. Through dialogue with peers they are helped to tackle the given problem and subsequently integrate that which had been incomprehensible and unfamiliar into their life-worlds.

Problem-based learning also enables students to explore and to develop their own tacit understandings. For example, the group can be a place in which students are not only able to connect with problems and concerns encountered external to themselves (for example, in practice placements, and when encountering problems or theory that is new to them), but are also able to make sense of inner inchoate understandings. However making sense of incoherence can be a precarious affair. O'Reilly (1989) has argued that there are risks involved in moving from experience that is incoherent to making public statements about one's self. For example, experience is often incoherent and in speaking of experience to others (publicly) is to risk sounding as if our experience is meaningless, contradictory and multiple (which it probably is). Experience is not something that can be tied into neat packages, and thus to speak of it is to risk being seen as stupid and incoherent, when it is in fact the reflections on those experiences that are incoherent. Meanings, particularly about prior experience and learning, seem to need eventually to become coherent in order that they can then be interpreted and subsequently valued. Problem-based learning programmes in which staff place value on prior experience must be prepared, therefore, to offer students the space and support to explore incoherence (and not just to resolve it prematurely). Such space and support extends the degree to which students are enabled not just to value prior experience but also to value the multiple and often contradictory meanings that emerge through it and from it. Reflection appears to play a key role in this process. This is particularly important for students where reflection on the learning process appears to be absent in lecture-based components of the course. Thus, problem-based learning seems, for many, to be the catalyst that prompts ways of working with and through their experience, often enabling them to link new experiences and knowledge to those of the past and thereby prompting new (more and less coherent) meanings.

Notions of problem-solving

The nature of problem-solving is to some degree connected with staff's view about the nature of knowledge (discussed below). However, the way in which problems are expected to be solved or managed appears to be connected with the profession and subject or discipline-base particular to the organizational context. For example, some problem scenarios tend to be limited by staff, so that students learn a particular body of knowledge and invariably produce a best answer that fits either with the tutor's agenda or purely with the particular material that is expected to be covered at the stage of the course. One staff member from engineering explained that:

> The students are in a position to be able to start it [the problem scenario] from previous knowledge and then they very quickly realise that there's more knowledge that they need and then we'd do a lecture. It all seems perfectly natural to them, they've spotted the need for this and of course the problems have been designed so that you present to them the whole knowledge base in what you believe to be a logical sequence. But they see it quite differently, it looks completely natural to them as if this happened to be a problem he thought up and it so happens that we need this theory. But if you look at the basic theory that I'm following it'll be dealt with in exactly the same order as it would have been on the conventional course.

Staff may also operate with the assumption that students need particular knowledge, for instance propositional knowledge, to solve problems. To recap, propositional knowledge is the kind of knowledge that includes discipline-based theories and concepts derived from bodies of knowledge, practical principles and generalizations, and specific propositions about particular cases, decisions or actions. Whereas personal knowledge, developed by Polanyi (1962), is the kind of knowledge that is deep seated and unformulated, it is the kind of knowledge that has become so part of our being that there is a taken-for-grantedness about it, it is *tacit*. Thus, where linear problem-solving models dominate the teaching-learning process, feedback (formal and informal) supplied by tutors tends to promote an over-emphasis on propositional knowledge, often at the expense of personal knowledge. What has been set up as problem-based learning can therefore become problem-solving learning because of the impact of staff's pedagogical stances on the forms of problem-solving and problem management that are allowed and disallowed. There are other instances where, although students are encouraged to explore problems and situations which do not lend themselves to tidy solutions, they are also encouraged to work within frameworks that guide both decision making and the kinds of knowledge on which they are likely to focus. For example, a number of staff involved in problem-based learning curricula have spoken of guiding students so that they do not reach beyond the second year stage (level 2 in England), while others have argued that knowledge and skills are not contestable within given contexts, such as in the case of drug administration (Savin-Baden, 1998). Yet there is a growing realization that in professional education the knowledge, practices and frameworks within which students work and learn are contestable, that different forms and areas of knowledge may contradict each other (Taylor, 1997) and, as Barnett has argued, 'the frameworks with which we interrogate the world . . . are multiplying' (Barnett, 1997b: 11).

Epistemological frameworks and priorities

The concept of an epistemological framework captures the idea that staff take up a particular position towards propositional knowledge. The position they take up guides the ways in which they design and implement curricula. Such frameworks impact upon the pedagogical stances students may be able to adopt within the curriculum because of the forms of problem-based learning on offer. Staff often see their role as providers and definers of knowledge and this narrow epistemological framework can prompt disjunction for students. For some students the delineation of knowledge by staff is something that is seen as helpful and acceptable as such strategies enable students to gain high marks. However, for other students the way in which knowledge is defined results in anger and frustration. Such students believe they should have the right to define knowledge on their own terms so that knowledge is constructed and contextual. They can therefore see themselves as creators rather than receivers of knowledge. Students may adopt different strategies for managing learning that connect with their perceived notions of staff's views of knowledge. These differences relate to emphasis put on the different forms of knowledge and the ways in which students are expected to explore this knowledge by staff and practitioners. For example, professions vary in the different emphasis that they put on personal and propositional knowledge (Barnett *et al.*, 1987).

Different notions of learning and knowledge within the institution, compared with those of industry or fieldwork or practice placements can cause conflict and subsequent disjunction for students. In such practice contexts there is often a focus on vocational relevance in which valid knowledge is only seen in terms of what it will enable the students to *do*. Thus, students are expected to demonstrate a level of understanding and competence that equates with supervising staff's memories of their own training at a similar stage. Other curricula where the ability to regurgitate theory is seen as paramount may encourage students to continue to acquire vast amounts of knowledge with the view that this is what will enhance their knowledge and understanding of the world. For example, cluttered syllabuses, along with the expectations of the professional bodies, and the focus on covering ground will be at odds for some students with the development of their learner identity. Yet the ways in which these kinds of barriers prompt disjunction in staff's and students' lives may force an interrogation of the theories and cultures that underpinned these disciplines.

Students' prior experiences of learning

For many students their prior experiences of learning and their view of themselves as learners lead them to assume that learning comprises rote memorization of facts. Difficulties they have experienced in learning in the past through didactic methods then results in a belief that it is necessarily they who are unsatisfactory, rather than the course or the system. Thus, for many their perception of themselves as failures or as individuals who find learning difficult are places where barriers to learning become evident. Students often speak about the way in which their prior experiences of learning in didactic programmes have been both frustrating and isolating experiences. However, when they first encounter problem-based learning they may find it difficult to see that their lived experiences, and those of others, are of worth. This, for many, is initially a source of disjunction. Students tend to value propositional knowledge provided by tutors more highly than that knowledge which emerges from their own experiences or from information researched by their peer group. For many students accepting that their own perspective is of value is problematic. The result is that often the information they provide for their peers is not deemed acceptable unless it has been checked or corrected by a tutor.

Through experiencing problem-based learning many students are challenged to revisit their perceptions of learning and of themselves. The disjunction emerging from this tends to prompt them to deconstruct, explore and transform their learner identity, and thus disjunction is central to this transformation process. For a number of students problem-based learning groups offer a context in which they feel able to explore their own learning and development. This is the beginning of a journey towards an understanding of their own stances and the domains they take up within them. However, the existence and nature of support available on the course, from staff or students, appears to be central to the extent to which this kind of self-discovery is experienced as positive or negative. Receiving support and encouragement from staff to evaluate the knowledge with which they are presented often results in disjunction for students. Forms of disjunction such as this are enabling because students experience support from staff who have asked for students' opinions and advice whilst simultaneously encouraging them to question and explore issues for themselves. Initially, many students feel uneasy and disoriented in dialogue with staff, often because their prior experiences of didactic teaching have silenced them into thinking that their opinions and former education are not of value. Disjunction then is characterized by students being voiceless in the face of knowledge (of whatever sort) and unable to see themselves as creators of knowledge who can value both subjective and objective strategies for knowing. Yet, simultaneously, students may use the groups not only to reflect on their difficulties in learning but also to explore and make sense of personal challenges. Opportunities for reflection within groups can offer oases of integration for some students; oases where transitional learning can and does take place. Thus personal reflection, along with reflection and discussion with others, equips many students to use skills and life experience in order to utilize the knowledge they have gained, and to reflect upon these processes. Groups are also locations in which reflection on disjunction being experienced can be supported and where transitions can be managed.

The context and the curriculum into which problem-based learning is placed

Although it is possible to argue, and many do, that there are more advantages to 'completely' problem-based programmes than hybrid versions (where only particular components or modules of the curriculum are problem-based), it is suggested here that what is also an important concern is faculty and managers' attitudes to the implementation of problem-based learning. The ways in which problem-based learning is adopted into the curriculum and portrayed to students will reflect the espoused values and values-in-use of staff involved. Where there is conflict between these espoused values and what happens in practice it is likely that disjunction will occur. For example, modular programmes in which the modular content is distinctly separate and is maintained within tight subject and discipline boundaries may cause students to have a fragmented experience of higher education. Here students will find it difficult to engage with problem-based learning because of the ways in which they are expected to cross discipline and subject boundaries for themselves when staff are still holding them as discrete entities.

Assessment is an area that is often problematic on programmes which espouse self-direction and learner-centred approaches because of issues of power and control between tutors and students. Therefore, it is in the context of assessment that it is often possible to see that opportunities for transitional learning can be lost. This is because when utilizing problem-based learning, staff make explicit their ideological claims regarding notions of self-direction and autonomy. This results in contradictions arising for students when these claims are not played out in practice and particularly when forms of assessment contradict these claims. For example, the form of assessment can encourage students to adopt methods of learning that ensure they pass the course with high grades, rather than to adopt learning approaches that would be in their best interests as an individual and a group member. Adopting individualistic methods may not be something in which many students personally believe. Neither do such methods fit particularly well with the forms of deep level learning encouraged through problem-based learning. As a result students may spend considerable time trying to discover covert criteria to enable them to pass the course. This confusion can be exacerbated further by the lack of information supplied about assessments and the inadequacy of feedback following assessed work.

Resources and funding

Reduced resources and funding in higher education in the late 1990s and early 2000s has been a catalyst to disjunction in programmes that do not use problem-based learning as well as those which do. This is due, in the main, to teaching larger numbers with the same or less resources. Drinan (1991) argued that constant awareness of the use and purposes of problem-based learning across the curriculum can lead to problem-based learning curricula that are no more expensive than traditional ones. There is still much controversy particularly with regard to library costs, classroom allocation and staff support for problem-based learning groups. However, Mennin and Martinez-Burrola (1990) studied the cost of problem-based learning compared with conventional curricula and demonstrated only very small differences. Furthermore, they also found that in problem-based learning curricula 70 per cent of faculty time was in contact with students, while on conventional courses 70 per cent of faculty time was in preparation for contact with students. From this it would seem then that the funding issues between problem-based learning and non-problem-based learning courses might just be a question of emphasis.

In the research I have presented here, the majority of students found the lack of library resources frustrating and disabling, but some found that poor resourcing actually enhanced creativity in learning and encouraged them to use themselves and their peers as learning resources. Simultaneously, several students also speculated as to whether in fact problem-based learning had been implemented to save staff time and to teach more students with less resources. In any problem-based learning programme it will be important to examine both the nature of support provided by staff, and the extent to which groups are or should be self-supporting, since peer relationships and staff–student relationships are critical in managing shifts away from disabling disjunction. It is important, therefore, that both staff and students in problem-based learning programmes value and utilize collaborative learning experiences and discuss the nature of support on offer.

Thus it can be seen from the documentation of these catalysts that issues which transcend different stances and which can also be connected with learner identity and learning context can result in ambiguity in students' lives. However, there are also different ways of managing disjunction which in themselves may affect the extent to which the experience of disjunction is educative or miseducative.

Dealing with disjunction: four key ways

Students deal with disjunction in a number of different ways which means that the conflict, ambiguity and incoherence experienced by individual students cannot be defined by distinctive characteristics, but there are some general trends. What seems to be apparent is that disjunction is dealt with by students, in one of four ways, through forms of decision making that are conscious and/or unconscious. Thus, students may opt to *retreat* from disjunction, to *temporize* and thus choose not to make a decision about how to manage it, to find some means to *avoid* it and thus create greater disjunction in the long term, or to *engage* with it and move to a greater or lesser sense of integration.

Retreat

In this position students who experience disjunction choose not to engage with the process of managing it. Here they want to avoid engaging with the struggles connected with disjunction and often retreat behind some form of excuse, which means that they do not engage with the personal or organizational catalyst to the disjunction. Students who retreat may also take up a particular position, entrench themselves within it and then reinforce the bunkers around that position.

Managing disjunction in this way can often result in a disabling experience with a tendency to blame others or the 'system' for what cannot be managed by the student. For example, one student at Stanage University believed that tutors were there to ensure that she learned what she was supposed to know in order to be a social worker. She retreated from engaging with disjunction because her sense of learner identity was threatened. Her view of tutors as authorities with the right answers meant that rather than risk learning knowledge for herself, she opted to reproduce information and ideas supplied and acquired through academics. Retreat appears to be more in evidence where a considerable focus is placed upon gaining propositional knowledge in other areas of the curriculum, which subsequently prompts disjunction between different and multiple knowledges. Barnett has argued that it 'is not that the sites of knowledge production are proliferating; it is that the academe's definitions of knowledge are increasingly challenged' (Barnett, 1997b: 3). This in turn can result in conflict for students about the nature of self-direction and autonomy within the programme, and often prohibits students from not only organizing their knowledge in a discriminating way, but also in developing the necessary self-critique that will enable them to engage with disjunction.

Temporizing

Students who do not directly retreat from disjunction may adopt an indecisive or time-serving policy. They acknowledge the existence of disjunction and also that they have to engage with it in order to enable an effective transition to take place, but they decide that it is preferable to postpone making any decision about how to manage it. Thus, there is, in the area in which the disjunction is occurring, a postponement of any activity. For example, Emily at Baslow valued the freedom in learning she experienced in the problem-based learning days. Yet she was uncomfortable about researching an issue whilst on a practice placement because she felt this met with disapproval by the nurses on the ward. Although Emily had managed disjunction that had occurred in the university learning context, she opted to temporize within the clinical setting, in order to avoid engaging with the role conflict she experienced between being a student and being a nurse. She postponed engaging with the challenge to her idealized notion of autonomous learning because of the barrier to this that she encountered in the practice setting.

Avoidance

In this situation students do not just temporize but adopt mechanisms that will enable them to find some way of circumventing the disjunction. The result will be that, although the student has found a means of bypassing the disjunction, this may have taken more effort than engaging with it, especially as in the long term, because of the nature of disjunction, they will still have to engage with disjunction in their life-world in order to avoid always becoming entrenched in this position.

For example, Rob was an English graduate who had worked as a residential worker before deciding to train to be a qualified social worker. He argued that there was a credibility gap between the portrayed role of tutors within the theoretical model of problem-based learning, which was presented to the students in the initial stages of the course, and the realities of their practice as tutors, facilitators and possibly even as social worker role models. Rob maintained that, even though tutors spoke of wanting to devolve power to the students, in practice they were either not prepared to devolve it or not capable of doing so. Rob's perspective reflects the fact that he believed that 'really useful knowledge' (Johnson, 1988) could only be gained when the exercise of power was diminished or removed (Usher and Edwards, 1994). The issue of power is rarely openly acknowledged in problem-based contexts, and it was Rob's recognition of the clear reality of this that prompted his reaction of anger and frustration towards tutors. This resulted in a disabling disjunction for Rob, which he chose to avoid by opting out of commitment to the group and to himself as a learner. Instead, he became increasingly dissatisfied with his own learning and performance on the course. He perpetually encountered disjunction in the same areas that he had continued to avoid, and it was not until a year later that he began to make sense of the difficulties he experienced in relation to his learner stances and learner identity in the context of engaging with his disjunction.

Engagement

Engaging with disjunction requires that students acknowledge its existence and also attempt to deconstruct the causes of disjunction by examining the relationship with both their internal and external worlds. Through this reflexive examination process students can engage with what has given rise to the disjunction and they are then enabled to shift towards a greater sense of integration either within the same domain or alternatively by adopting a different one.

Bill's prior experience of didactic teaching methods at Lembert, which brought with it the view that he was expected to learn and cope with difficulties alone, resulted in an initial confusion and subsequent disjunction about the process of learning through groups. Bill could not understand how he could learn through discussing the problem scenarios or how students' differing approaches to problem-solving could possibly produce a cohesive group and an effective answer. Yet the disjunction he experienced as a result of this confusion was enabling because of the way in which he was subsequently able not only to make sense of the problems and relate them to his prior experience, but also through this process to learn to 'construct his own voice'.

Belenky *et al.* (1986) used the metaphor of voice to encapsulate the way in which women in their study made sense of their experiences as learners. Students who engage with disjunction tend to speak not of constructing a voice, but of 'gaining a voice' (Savin-Baden, 1996), as a way to depict an intellectual and ethical process whereby the development of a sense of voice, mind and self are interlinked. The ability to 'construct a voice' encompasses the way in which students speak of engagement with their disjunction and the transitions which often ensue. Constructing a voice is thus a dynamic process through which construction, deconstruction and reconstruction occurs. For example, students may be able to 'speak for themselves' in some circumstances and not others, yet there is not always a conscious realization of voice (or lack of it). Students perhaps are able to speak within their peer group and problem-based learning group but are not always able to interact with tutors whom they see as experts. For students the ability to articulate their own confusions around disjunction often results in a shift towards a greater consciousness and/or understanding of their learner identity.

Conclusion

It is vital to see disjunction as central to learner experience, particularly as problem-based learning seems to set up the possibility for disjunction in students' lives. It is also critical for staff and students to realize that disjunction may not just occur in relation to learning, which is seen by students to be meaningful. Thus, both staff and students in problem-based learning programmes need to be made aware of different forms of disjunction so that they can explore the ways in which this may affect the practical out-working of the problem-based learning programme, both in the context of the institution and the context of people's lives. Furthermore, it is important that disjunction is managed effectively. Mechanisms should be in place so that disjunction *can* be managed, and in ways in which it *is* or *becomes* enabling, so that the burden of responsibility for managing that disjunction is not left wholly with the students.

The ability to engage with and manage disjunction is a complex process that involves transitions. Transitions involve both critical reflection and critical self-reflection and can involve shifts towards or away from a sense of integration or disjunction in different learner stances. The ways in which transitions occur and the processes whereby new and/or old perspectives are affirmed or discarded through experiencing different forms of disjunction is now explored in detail.

7

Managing Transition

This chapter explores the nature of transitions that occur in the context of problem-based learning and that arise as a result of disjunction. Although I argue here that transitions are not something for which individuals should take total responsibility, it is often the case in educational environments that it is the students who do ultimately take responsibility for managing disjunction and the resulting transitions that occur. It is perhaps important to note at the outset that transitions are multidirectional and emerge from the complex interactions of students personally, pedagogically and inter-actionally. Thus, transitions are not seen to arise specifically out of issues connected with the intellect, the maturity and overall competence of the student.

As discussed in earlier chapters, problem-based learning often prompts transitions in learning and thus if students are offered opportunities to engage with and manage transitions through problem-based learning, then it is likely that this approach to learning will be appealing to students, tutors and employers. Managing transitions effectively will mean that students develop the complexity skills (Robertson, 1998) that higher education and society at large seem to require. Complexity skills are the advanced skills which go beyond key skills and subject skills in a qualification framework, such as the capacity to work in complex and ambiguous contexts and to solve and manage problems in ways that transcend conventional lines of thinking. Thus, we will have students who can not only transfer skills but also critique perspectives, including their own, manage uncertain and often ambiguous situations and be flexible individuals who are attuned to market forces.

The nature of transitions and an examination of the extent to which they are seen to be educative for students will be explored first. The latter section of the chapter deals with issues connected with the effective management of transitions and offers some suggestions about how staff, students and course designers might put these into practice.

The nature of transitions

Transition is used here to denote shifts in learner experience caused by a challenge to the person's life-world. Transitions occur in particular areas of students' lives, at different times and in distinct ways. The notion of transitions carries with it the idea of movement from one place to another and with it the necessity of taking up a new position in a different place. Leaving the position and entering the transitions may also be fraught with difficulties, which may result in further disjunction for the student. Thus, transitions can often be difficult and disturbing and yet simultaneously be areas where personal change takes place.

In the framework of Dimensions of Learner Experience, transitions were constituted as the process whereby new and/or old perspectives were reviewed or discarded through experiencing different forms of disjunction. This kind of critical reflection and critical self-reflection can involve shifts towards or away from a sense of disjunction in different learner stances. For example, any transition may result in someone being able to make greater or lesser sense of their lives. In the context of problem-based learning, students' concepts of learning and knowledge are often challenged because they are expected to be researchers of and creators of knowledge in ways that few have encountered in their prior learning experiences. Thus, problem-based learning can be a significant challenge to students who expect learning to be discipline-based even if the knowledge being learned coalesces around a problem scenario. Students in higher education, particularly in lecture-based programmes, rarely receive opportunities to integrate knowledge across disciplines and rarely expect to be asked to do so. Furthermore, it would seem from research into students' learning that students still construe learning tasks as predominantly assimilating and reproducing material supplied by academics, rather than engaging with what is meaningful for them and framing experience for themselves (Entwistle, 1987; Gibbs, 1992; Barnett, 1994).

Transcending discipline boundaries may be difficult to manage if students see knowledge as essentially propositional rather than connected to their learner or pedagogic identity. Through problem-based learning students can become critically aware of new learning needs, which arise from the challenge to dimensions of their current learner experience. This awareness results in the adoption of a different domain, which has different meanings from the previous one they have taken up. Transitions are not always worthwhile experiences for students, and their impact will depend on each individual student and circumstance. However, what is common to all students is the move both towards and away from attaining an integrated sense of self, within different stances, at different moments in time. Furthermore, transitions are not linear but recursive. They involve revisiting and redefining knowledge and experiences, rather than necessarily refining them, although the latter may also occur.

Yet to talk of transition as an abstract concept, divorced from the lives of students, would be to deny the centrality and vitality of voice in transitional learning. For transitions to be educative experiences it is important that students are facilitated in moving beyond inchoate and tacit understandings of their transitions and that educators realize the means whereby they can ensure that transitions are ultimately educative for students.

Transitions as educative experiences

Much is documented on the notion of transitions but there is very little documented about how transitions occur, what prompts them or whether they are worthwhile or educative (see, for example, Perry, 1970; Mezirow, 1981; Taylor, 1986; Taylor, 1997).

Meaning making is often discussed as something which is equipping, encouraging and all too often sounds easy and accessible. While many would argue that to make sense of an issue, concern or situation is something which is of value, too often the cost of engaging in such a process is ignored. By acknowledging that transitions have their costs personally, pedagogically, and interactionally, and hence have a life cost, staff and students' values will not be lost amidst the learning process; for example, values about what it is that holds meaning for individuals and what it is that frames belief. Perry (1981) has argued for the practice of 'allowing for grief' in the process of growth and development in learning. By allowing for grief it will be possible for educators to help students to acknowledge and come to terms with the sense of loss. That done it will then be required that students are helped to take further steps towards transcending their knowing and encouraged to develop new meanings in order that they are prevented from shifting towards disabling disjunction, isolation and alienation.

If educators can offer students space for learning and for managing their grief in the transitional process then transitions can be managed, not necessarily without pain or loss, but at least with meaningful and realistic support that helps students to legitimize their experiences. Whilst it would be possible to trace issues that emerged from the data which enable and disable the transitional process for individual students, the list would be complex, unwieldy and would risk over-simplifying and stereotyping the complexity of individual students' experiences. What I offer instead are a number of assumptions, which stem from students' and tutors' expectations within a learning environment, that can both facilitate and prevent transitions taking place:

- students can and will take responsibility for their learning
- students can make sense of the relationship and interaction between personal and propositional knowledge
- the exploration and (re)building of identity is valued and rewarded and is a key process in professional education
- life experience is of value and to be built on
- learning through interaction is of value to teachers and to learners.

Thus, in order that transitions are educative it is vital that students and teachers acknowledge, engage with and make explicit these issues. They can be classified under three headings: legitimated experience, authentic dialogue and identity (re)building.

Legitimated experience

Legitimated experience captures the idea that students learn to value the worth of their experience. Students in a variety of learning contexts find it difficult to take seriously their prior experiences. It is often through realizing the value of their experience that they are enabled to manage disjunction and subsequent transition. It is the very process of legitimating their own experience which enables learners to acknowledge and interpret the text of their experiences, and thus reconstruct prior notions of legitimate forms of learning, knowledge and personal experience. Whilst the concept of legitimated experience can be seen as important for transition to take place, inevitably it can be the very prompt for a transition away from disjunction and towards a sense of integration. Experience seemed to be legitimated for students in the context of problem-based learning through a number of particular issues. For example, Nicola was a student for whom the nurturing of confidence and the receiving of support from group members enabled her to both perceive and develop a greater sense of her own potential. Nicola was an English and Drama graduate who had worked in a children's home for four years before going to Stanage to study social work. She described herself as someone who did not have very strong opinions, but believed that, through problem-based learning, her values had been challenged and changed. Nicola talked about her transition from a caterpillar to a butterfly as a process of metamorphosis. Change seemed to have occurred for Nicola, not because she was lacking in opinions and values, but because previously she had felt that she had little confidence or knowledge in substantiating them.

> I think this course has enabled me to form some opinions about things. Things that are very fundamental really . . . We had this discussion today about disability and access, and if it's not something you've ever really thought about, when you start to think about it, its absolutely ridiculous that people can't get into shops or get on a bus. And this building is appalling, appallingly inaccessible. So it's right to have strong opinions. But its not just – they haven't come out of nowhere, they've had to have evolved because I've had to learn about it. And I think it's to do with really, really having to look at things, you know, and to be able to back up your opinions, substantiate them.

Nicola's belief was that through being challenged to discover and reflect on issues she had been enabled to develop her own opinions for herself and to learn to express herself, which had ultimately led her to believe that her experience and opinions were to be valued since they were legitimized by others and ultimately herself.

Chris's experience stood in contrast to Nicola's. Chris, studying mechanical engineering at Gimmer, was a school leaver whose experience of working in industry during his summer holidays had given him a practical understanding of engineering problems. He had hoped that the problem-based learning module would allow him to think and explore in a way he had been unable to during the lecture-based components of the degree, where he felt bored and constrained by having to learn in a mechanistic way. For Chris the meaning of learning in a problem-based manner lay in its capacity to facilitate students' independence in thinking, yet he believed that his perception of problem-based learning was at odds with that of the tutor:

> You are told to go along to (problem-based learning) tutorials and basically you're told in those tutorials what they think you should be doing to get the problem solved. I mean you can't get anywhere without a little bit of guidance . . . but it does seem to me the big drawback to this is you being told what you should do and that if you come up with any answers that's not what they've got then its wrong. And I don't feel engineering's about that, engineering is an open-ended question.

Chris wanted to cultivate a greater personal awareness and a deeper sense of exploration and engagement with what was being learned, but he found tutors' attitudes limited his opportunities to become personally involved and prevented him from using the resources he possessed. Chris argued against this, he believed that his own perspective was relevant and felt angry that tutors saw themselves as having the right to delineate knowledge and experience and, as a consequence, de-legitimize his own.

Authentic dialogue

The nature of learning within academic institutions is invariably bound up with reward for the individual rather than for group achievement. Much of the 'real' learning that occurs through problem-based learning transpires through group interaction, but this is seldom rewarded in academic terms. Students tend to articulate 'real' learning in terms of learning that has personal meaning for them, they speak of 'making sense', 'connecting' and 'seeing things in a new way', all within the context of the group. For many students, learning that occurs in relation to the group process actually has more meaning than the learning which is rewarded in terms of marks and grades.

For some students, dialogue in the groups is a process through which they discover and develop themselves, whilst for others dialogue is anticipated as an opportunity through which values can be deconstructed and reconstructed. Therefore, dialogue may be central to transitions being managed effectively but in different ways for students. For example, some students see the opportunity for dialogue as prompting progress towards a deeper understanding of personal and corporate values and relationships, which brings with it opportunities for personal development. Thus, students use the group process to make sense of and challenge issues connected with identity, which they can then relate to the wider social context in which they live and work.

There is a need to emphasize, in programmes that use problem-based learning, the value of dialogue within groups for enabling individuals to reflect on prior experiences, connect with their life-world and facilitate making sense of current or previous concerns not formerly understood. Integration between the interaction of learners and the learning context seems to be an issue that particularly appears to facilitate a validation of individuals through the group. This integration appeared to be particularly evident at Lembert for two reasons. First, many of the students at Lembert had previously experienced didactic programmes where learning was an individualistic and disparate process, an issue that was also raised by students at Gimmer. Thus, learning with and through others was seen by many as a positive experience compared with prior experiences. Second, the opportunity to learn 'informally' because the cohort had a dedicated room was something that was seen by many to demonstrate the value placed by staff on group work. Students at Lembert saw learning as a community activity, a social experience where learning did not just occur in the formal group work, but also occurred during lunch breaks and at the pub. This sociality in learning promoted individual students' self-development through the student community.

Students across the sites believed that learning in a group had given them the understanding that in collaborative groups it was necessary to both give and receive support so that members could work cohesively. Mike, at Lembert, captured the way in which many students talked of this: 'You can see from working as a team the help you can give within your group to some of the members that may be struggling about a particular subject. You get self-fulfilment 'cos you've helped them in an area and then you know that perhaps some time in the future they'll help you.' It was evident that the community spirit prompted through group work built a sense of trust and self-validation, which enabled students not only to value others but to also value and share their own knowledge and experience.

Identity (re)building

Learner identity, and changes within it, which often emanate through transitions do not seem, overall, to occur in isolation. Problem-based learning appears to prompt, for some students, a form of identity building through the group. What was apparent were not only transitions that took place across stances and domains but the significance of transitions *between* people within the learning context. It was often these latter transactions, in which dialogue was central, that became the arena for recognizing and developing learner identity:

> Through face-to-face interaction within these groups [*of generalized and significant others*] we continually confirm or change our private and public roles and the way we understand reality. The groups to which one belongs, as they are composed of several subjective realities, represent segments of objective reality which are relevant to one's subjective understanding of life.
>
> (Wildemeersch, 1989: 64)

Students' reflections on their own roles within groups, the roles of other group members and the relationship between group members seemed to force individual students to consider the ways in which they relate, and want to relate, to others. It also prompted them to question the extent to which they do and do not belong to the group. This process, in which learning is central, results in a challenge to learner identity through self-doubt and self-discovery. Thus, each student's experience of problem-based learning is bound up with individual and personal concerns.

For example, Ian's pedagogical stance was linked to the values he saw as being implicit within both knowledge provided by academics, and experiences and knowledge with which he was supplied in practice, both before commencing the course and on practice placements. Ian argued that problem-based learning offered students opportunities, though somewhat limited, for exploring their perspectives and values in relation to the social work values that they were being encouraged to adopt:

> I think where the difficulty is, is that the problem-based learning course hasn't taken into account that there's a continual interaction between your own experiences and your particular Social Work philosophy or perspective. And that if you're actually going to talk about your experiences within the group work context or whatever it is, you have to take into account that there is a Social Work philosophy which develops out of that, which also affects the way you work.

For Ian, learning was the process of critically evaluating personal knowledge in the light of propositional knowledge. Encountering other students' views of the world had encouraged him to become increasingly self-reflective and revisit his own assumptions and values. Yet he was concerned about the extent to which knowledge could be legitimately explored in the context of practice. Within social work practice there were dominant values that were seen to be unchallengeable, and for students to become increasingly reflexive within their pedagogical stance it was vital to understand that knowledge and learning was related to more than discipline-based values, learning facts and passing the course. Ian explained his perspective: 'So it's [*learning*] not necessarily that much to do with facts. I think you do need facts, you do need to understand the issues to be worked through, but on the other hand it's more important to look at the way experiences you've had in these areas have affected your approach.' Critically evaluating prior experiences of social work practice was vital to seeing learning and epistemology as flexible entities, and thus being able to evaluate critically and to challenge concepts, ideas and assumptions.

Enabling transition

Students' stories demonstrated that there were particular issues which facilitated students' transitions in learning. The notion and experience of transition, emerging from disjunction, appears to prompt an interrogation of traditional perspectives of learner, learning, the learning context, professions, institutions, etc. What is required is an examination of what these transitions *mean* for tutors and students, in order that problem-based learning does not become one of the approaches to learning which is increasingly condemned as an approach that offers naive understandings of learning processes.

Transitions resulting from disjunction force an interrogation of the achievements and experiences of the past in relation to what is presently occurring for the students. Thus, during interviews with students, critical self-reflection demonstrated the ways in which they had become enabled through the process of transitions occurring. The following section details suggestions for those using forms of experiential learning, including problem-based learning, to facilitate transitions for students.

Setting up challenges to students' life-worlds

Whilst I argue here that educators cannot and should not coerce students into personal and pedagogical development it is important that the role of education is seen to be that of creating opportunities for transitions to occur. If, as Jarvis (1987) suggested, one of the most significant aspects of teaching adults is first to raise meaningful and relevant questions in adults' minds so that they can respond to the disjunction that has been created, then the opportunities for experiencing disjunction are those which are effected in some sense through the institutions themselves. Jarvis's perspective, however, raises questions about whether staff are in fact able to set up situations to promote disjunction, whether it is desirable that they do and, if disjunction then occurs, whether they are in fact able to respond. Weil has argued that it is students rather than staff or the institution who 'carry the burden of responsibility for managing disjunction' (Weil, 1989: 140).

Staff therefore have a responsibility to recognize and validate students' experiences of disjunction and to facilitate students in connecting with and engaging in effective transitional experiences.

Offering space for learning, reflecting and meaning making

Reflection is the process through which social beings examine themselves within a cultural context. It is a process whereby the frameworks by which people live and operate are challenged and transcended in the act of evaluating the world and themselves and even that very act of self-evaluation. Students develop and gain an increasing sense of their identity as through the processes involved in transitions they meet new barriers to learning that emerge in each new domain they enter (and in some cases also in each domain they leave). For instance, they will meet new barriers by moving away from forms of learning characterized by received knowledge or in attempting to understand the world differently at a different level of strategic pedagogy. They will develop and adopt the kind of learning characterized by pedagogical autonomy and constructed knowledge in which learning becomes a project of self-discovery and in which reflection is central to this process of becoming.

Yet opportunities for individual and corporate reflection can only emerge within curricula where the belief in reflection is not only espoused but is undertaken in practice. Such belief can only emerge from the premise that independent enquiry and reflection on one's life-world is worthwhile and to be valued within professions and academic institutions. Weil argues

> Space for learning implies opportunities to reflect on individual and collective goals, within the boundaries and possibilities of a particular programme or subject area. Enabling teachers and groups can go a long way to counteract the impact of disjunction arising from forces that seem outside the bounds of one's personal agency, and to create an oasis of integration in which the experience of other kinds of disjunction can be made sense of and more effectively managed.
>
> (Weil, 1989: 140)

Furthermore, reflection on one's previous domain can enhance the perceived educational value of the actual process of transition. Once a shift to a new domain has been undertaken and consolidated, a transition to a previous domain will often be more costly personally (although not necessarily pedagogically if, for example, a student can improve his overall degree grade by adopting strategic methods). This is because once a transition is made to the new domain, reflection on the old leads to seeing it afresh – and invariably as no longer useful, applicable or helpful to the current position taken up in the new domain.

Encouraging students to transcend personal, pedagogical and political boundaries

All too often tutors espouse the notion that students are to be encouraged in the formulation of their own judgements, in challenging those of the academe and in evaluating the practice of the profession for which they are training. Although at one level tutors may offer such encouragements and sometimes support students in this process, all too often students adopt or revert to the developments of identities and strategies which will affirm academic and professional agenda. Assessment mechanisms, covert agenda and shifts to so-called efficiency in learning can all teach students to read the academe as a forum in which the ultimate goal is to beat the system. Instead, students should be fostered in developing themselves, and in cultivating learner identities, in ways that will both challenge and enhance the interrelated worlds of theory and practice.

Enabling the development of critique

The site of transitional learning, that is learning which occurs as a result of critical reflection on shifts (transitions) which have taken place for the students personally (including viscerally), pedagogically and/or interactionally, would seem to be the ideal garden in which to grow and develop critique. It would seem that many tutors in higher education, professionally based or otherwise, are in the market garden business. Here they nurture young shoots as cheaply as possible and expect that whatever (manure?) they throw at them, students will develop themselves despite the system – so that the tutor can take the credit. Cynical, perhaps, but what must not be lost sight of is the way in which much of what is offered to students does not in fact encourage the kinds of thinking, reasoning and reflecting that would seem to be at the heart of approaches such as problem-based learning. If tutors are to be in the critique business then their professional frameworks and the development of professional identities must be bound not by discipline-based knowledge, critical thinking skills and the like. Instead, their frameworks must be negotiable, and their courses should be places where transactional dialogue can take place, and gardens where 'stirring dull roots with spring rain' (Eliot, 1954) is the work of the day.

Critique is to be seen as a form of criticism of the discipline (Barnett, 1997a). Thus, a notion of critique brings with it the transcendence of the discipline and a reflexivity around that very transcendence in which differing views are celebrated. Barnett (1997a) has offered us a model of criticality in which he suggested that what is required are three interconnected levels of criticality, namely critical action, critical self-reflection and critical reason. These three interconnected strands offer us a map for developing not just critique in students but for developing critical beings with complexity skills for the globalized age. Missing from Barnett's analysis are two things. First, the practical means of undertaking these shifts in a system of higher education in which more boundaries are put up than brought down, particularly when critique is on offer. Second, the understanding that some students, and indeed staff, may not see the shift from critical thinking, through critical thought to critique, as upwardly developmental and necessarily worthwhile for students.

It is apparent that where opportunities for movement towards critique are possible for students, they are not always seen as desirable, because of the personal and professional conflicts that might emerge in attempting to transcend disciplinary frameworks (Savin-Baden, 1996). What is required is a means of encompassing all the components of criticality into ways that support students, which offer different modes of learning that encourage criticality and which enable students to make informed choices about the transitions they make with a realistic understanding of the costs entailed and the reality of the support on offer. It is only then that it will be possible to have Barnett's model of criticality as a means of developing a critical being with complexity skills – who *has* choice.

Conclusion

The real questions here are not just about how theoretical positions are changed in higher education or how courses are designed including those which are problem-based, so that they develop critique in students. The real questions are about how this is played out in practice beyond the ivory towers of books such as this. It is too easy to sit and write about challenging frameworks and exploring differing ways of seeing the world, but the means of making it happen are also required. The next chapter explores the notion of critique in greater detail and compares the theory of criticality with practical issues connected with courses that use problem-based learning. For example, for many students it is not the level of each stage of the course that is at issue but the steepness of the slope. Levels of expectation and outcome are common across all courses that educate the world's future professionals. It seems that few staff who have adopted problem-based learning have engaged with the complex affair of expecting first year students only to be at the level of describing and discussing issues within submitted work. This goes against the grain of problem-based learning where students are in reality expected, by facilitators, to at least use critical thought as they engage with their initial scenario in their first term.

8

As Good as it Gets?

A nursing tutor looks at the module objectives in the course document and turns to me with a puzzled frown. He tells me that he cannot possibly ask students to analyse a case scenario and identify their learning needs because analysis only happens in the third year of the course. This is not the first time he has felt confused about the relationship between academic levels and problem-based learning. His confusion reflects the paradoxical nature of higher education in the face of competencies and learning outcomes – and he knows this.

The image of this tutor is a reminder, for me, of a third-year undergraduate occupational therapy student whose quest to understand and interpret knowledge in relation to herself is silenced by those tutors whose thinking she challenges. As she wades her way, with joy, through Dewey and Mezirow and exclaims that Boud's thinking on reflective practice is 'underdeveloped in places' the challenge is to support her as she writes beyond academic level three. She has begun to challenge professional frameworks and transcend discipline boundaries, she has learned the value of transactional dialogue but she is constrained by the professional knowledge base in which she works and learns. What will be whispered in the corridors of professional power is that this kind of writing, this sort of critical thought, is too much, too uncomfortable and possibly even unprofessional.

A few weeks later a physicist and an engineer argue over whether students have to cover a given body of knowledge in order to be safe practitioners. Their arguments centre not on whether students can use this knowledge but on the age-old argument that as long as students have been given the information in a lecture then they, as tutors, have done their job and have been responsible. The point, as far as the physicist is concerned, is that covering material and passing examinations is the only way to ensure students learn what they, the experts, think they need to know. The engineer on the other hand does not want students with a kit of unusable theories. He would rather they had complexity skills.

For many these will be familiar stories. They are stories that raise a multitude of issues about the choices being made within curricula because of mechanistic and outcomes-based approaches to learning. As academics ask themselves what it means for students to be life-long learners in the face of competencies and academic levels, and also reflect upon the rapidity of change in higher education, the ultimate question for many will become 'what if this is as good as it gets?' Higher education, it seems, has been set up to allow for incoherence, an examination of knowledges and to sustain a diversity of human experience. Looking ahead it is possible to see an increase in the remit and thus the breadth of higher education that many will find unsustainable. For if a virtual university is to be filled with students who are learning in fragmented and diverse ways across cyber space, many tutors will fall by the wayside. This may be because they are unable to keep up with the demands of change, the inhumanity of voice mail and learning packages or because they still believe in the notion of a university whose key underpinnings are the legitimization of knowledge and truth. Many academics in the UK are expected to manage, on the one hand, high research outputs and market-led competency-based teaching such as National Vocational Qualifications (NVQ), to Masters level (?), and, on the other, the use of experience for learning and students engaged in transactional dialogue.

At the same time, the complex interrelationship of professional education with higher education results in circumstances whereby multiple systems and ideologies can be seen to be pulling against one another. The changes within professional curricula have been influenced not only by the often stringent regulations of professional bodies but also by the desire to marry the curricula outcomes for education for the professions with those of the university structure. The ultimate aim has been to create programmes in which there are discrete modules that are defined in terms of levels, outcomes and Credit Accumulation and Transfer (CAT) points so that students can opt for different modules not only within the same university but also across different universities. If two modules were evaluated, which cover the same propositional knowledge, the same skills and attitudes and expect the same learning outcomes at level one, then under the current UK-wide university system it might be assumed that there would be little difference between the two. Students, in theory, should thus be able to negotiate a transfer between one course and the next. The only real difference that can be seen is the mode of delivery, the process. It is the only thing that ultimately distinguishes one course from another, but in many ways this very difference could prove disastrous for the student. A first year student who has undertaken a didactic programme of lectures will be expected to be able to describe issues and experiences or present 'received knowledge' (Belenky *et al.*, 1986). Yet, if she transfers to a problem-based learning programme, the demands will be different even at the outset of an undergraduate course. The demands will be for critical thought and with it the ability to analyse, synthesize and use well-developed problem-solving skills. So far this seems to have been little examined or acknowledged in undergraduate curricula.

Although this new currency may mean more freedom and choice for students, it brings with it similar problems to that of the *euro*, that of value, perceived or real. There is a sense and an expectation, then, that 20 CAT points will be a constant but the relative strength of such currency will oscillate depending on confidence in the market. Teaching quality assessment, research ratings and high calibre staff will all affect the market value, even if in fact the course in a high status university is not as good as the analogous course at the college down the road. The outcome measures that are designed to improve the quality of research and teaching, and perhaps most importantly students' experiences of learning, may be the very things prompting discontinuity rather than enabling the process of learning. Much has already been written about the relationship between professional education and higher education but it still seems to be a rather unhappy marriage. Eraut (1994) offers a map of types of professional knowledge that he sees as central to professional education. This map comprises propositional knowledge, personal knowledge and process knowledge. He defined propositional knowledge as that which emerges out of professional action and defines the knowledge base of the profession in terms of discipline-based knowledge and concepts, practical principles and frameworks. Eraut defined personal knowledge as that acquired through social interaction and undertaking tasks. It has little overt connection with learning and tends to remain at the level of basic impressions, or in other words it is the kind of knowledge that emerges from experience and is somewhat inchoate in the professional context. Finally, Eraut suggested that the notion of process knowledge can be seen as understanding how to undertake the processes that contribute to professional action. These are the processes that comprise and describe what professionals do, and these include understanding and using propositional knowledge.

What Eraut's map does not seem to be able to sustain is the interaction of personal and propositional knowledge as defined by the personal stance of the student. For if tutors are to develop in their students learner identities rather than pedagogic identities, then they must seek to develop in students a sense of self that enables them to see the critical ambiguity between personal and propositional knowledge in the context of professional life. Furthermore, although Eraut's map of professional knowledge (1994) has been helpful in making sense of the complex interrelated issues, it does not help staff to find innovative and creative ways of managing the dynamics between higher education and professional education. However, it is not just a map (or a compass) that is required, or even a bridge. What is needed is something new and different that will fill this chasm, something which will embrace and transcend the dominant cultures of higher education and professional agenda, a new transdisciplinary constellation that offers not just theoretical ideals but practical out workings of these ideals. It is possible to undertake this on two interrelated levels: first, that of public theories and personal interpretations, and, second, that of academic boundaries and professional territories (mapped in Figure 8.1). With problem-based learning

Figure 8.1 Dynamic issues in higher education and professional education

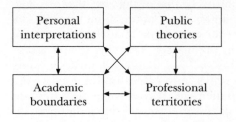

as a unifying framework that allows for fragility and incoherence it may then be possible to create a structure in which diversity in learning and across contexts is managed and celebrated rather than ignored and marginalized. The notion of a particular concept of problem-based learning as a means of managing this gap will be the main focus of the next chapter.

These issues and their interrelationship will now be examined before considering the ways in which the chasms between them might be addressed.

Necessary ambiguities

Public theories capture the idea that despite individual differences within a society there are moral codes and particular views to which that society in general subscribes. Inevitably there is a constant state of flux, and boundaries shift according to societal trends and the influence of media and popular philosophy, but there tend to be codes about human rights and responsibilities from which professional codes of conduct and professional behaviour emerge. These public theories also influence, however covertly, what is expected of a professional, of whatever sort. This can be seen in the dichotomous problems to which many in the nursing profession are subjected as they continue to support a remuneration system (they know should be changed) because of the public outcry against nurses who go on strike. They have, it is said, a vocation, and as such they are expected not to complain and to give their lives for the good of the community. Public theories, however much they are denied, do influence professional behaviour and professional education. Public theories also spill over into personal interpretations.

Personal interpretations stem from individual beliefs and are played out not just through the values that are held but also through the way these values are interpreted in practice in the context of life and work. Values are seldom made explicit in university documents, although they are increasingly to be seen in the corporate world, where to make values explicit is seen as a means of defining the fundamentals of the relationship between people within an organization and their relationship with the world beyond that organization. In having a set of core values and making them overt, supermarkets and blue chip companies expect that their policies and procedures will be clear and that decision making and performance can be assessed against them. The ways in which value statements are used in these companies are often outcome driven and thus miss the complexity and difficulties of relationship within them. The principle of exploring values is a good one, yet, in the context of higher education, is this discussion raised? It is evident that within any given curriculum the way in which lecturers interpret and present material reflects their values and personal interpretations of what it is important for students to learn. Although they may at one level be bound by modular descriptors and core professional skills, what tutors present to the students are actually their personal interpretations.

Academic boundaries, which secure the identity of the academe itself, are continually on the move. Barnett (1997b) has argued that in an age of supercomplexity there can be no borders, but simultaneously he points out that those wanting to become a university will have to meet predetermined criteria. So while many are arguing for a different kind of university where diversity is the name of the game, there are still those who continue to erect more boundaries (for example, the codes of practice and approved pool of external examiners as defined by Sir Ron Dearing and his committee, NCIHE, 1997). There continue to be those today who would still argue for a university whose function is the production, legitimation and dissemination of knowledge. That is not to deny that liberal education such as this can offer students opportunities for meaningful learning. Yet there is today still a tension between an autonomous system of higher education whose focus is to preserve and extend society's dominant culture, and a form of higher education that is more vocationally relevant. Although the latter form may be increasingly accountable to the public and State, it brings with it an emphasis on the development of personal qualities and skills for life and work, as well as focusing on issues of student learning in new ways. Academic boundaries are becoming subsumed into a culture of relativism where anything goes and what counts for academia and what counts as knowledge is more broadly defined and more deeply critiqued than in former years. Many academics still feel that they have to point out and demonstrate that their definitions of knowledge matter, but do they? Perhaps the academic boundaries are the academics themselves, those whose espoused theories are denied by their theories-in-use. There are those who become so bound by the red tape of university procedure that they cannot free themselves from these bonds, which ultimately offer legitimation. They therefore fail to take up opportunities for (re)defining themselves in relation to their life-world and the corporate community.

This kind of position can be seen too in the professional territories that guard the access to process and propositional knowledge as outlined by Eraut (1994). These particular territories are defined as those areas of knowledge and skills that are differentiated specifically by a profession, and are seen to be owned and bounded by that profession. It is expected that other professions will recognize and acknowledge this ownership, for example the professional knowledge base of physiotherapy, which may have components that overlap into occupational therapy, osteopathy, sports sciences and nursing, defines what constitutes physiotherapy as a subject area. There are those too who still support a notion that each profession has its knowledge base (for example Barnett, 1997a; Eraut, 1994). Nevertheless, it is hardly possible to specify a knowledge base in relation to any kind of qualified competent practitioner when knowledge is not a constant – except that it is in a constant state of change. What is more at issue is the definition of understanding of professional frameworks and professional identities. But I will return to this. The difficulty of arguing for the concept of a knowledge base is that propositional knowledge becomes a foundational concept on which all other knowledge is built. Problem-based learning turns arguments such as this on its head. One of the difficulties associated with problem-based learning is in its notion of knowledge. Margetson (1991a) has suggested that the assumption that 'knowledge is certain' persists in higher education and that the assumed link between certainty and knowledge is used to justify didactic teaching. Consequently problems may be limited in two ways. First, knowledge may be generated through the solving of problems, but if they are real problems (those to which solutions are *not known*), then this type of activity is expected to be a matter for research rather than teaching and learning. Second, problems used in teaching and learning are of a special sort. The purpose of these problems is to test students' understanding of what has been taught, which means essentially that they are not real problems, since the solutions are already known. This atomistic conception of knowledge results in teaching becoming an act of putting students right and higher education becomes, through 'technicism', about teaching students to achieve given ends.

Methods of experiential learning such as problem-based learning therefore bring to the fore the problem of what actually counts as knowledge and who makes the decisions about what counts and what does not. The current situation is complex not only because of the forms of knowledge that are deemed to be acceptable within professions, but also because of the ways in which professions define the kinds of behaviours that are acceptable within that profession: 'there is in every profession a kind of bootlegging, in which the student, unwittingly or not, acquires from non-official vendors the ideas, values, and ways of behaving and thinking that are attributed, sometimes legitimately and sometimes not, to the profession' (Olesen and Whittaker, 1968: 8). It seems, therefore, that an understanding is needed about how students accommodate and integrate facets of role and self; how they see themselves as nurses, physiotherapists, lawyers, engineers as well as laity; how they learn to be aware of being aware; and how students manage the vicissitudes of professional and academic institutions.

The concept of 'turning experience into learning' is often spoken of in these days of reflective practice and experiential learning. The innovative work of Boud *et al.* (1985) has challenged many to consider and reconsider the importance of a student's experience in the process of learning but it is possible to see this from a different angle. Students may do the reverse and seek to turn learning into experience. For example, patterns of learning developed through competency-based and skill-based learning can result in a notion of professional life governed by means-end solutions, formulaic practices and a lack of sound professional judgement. Although, initially, for novices this may be seen as a helpful and enabling process, the long-term cost is of setting a pattern for professional life characterized by non-reflective practices and modes of thinking that barely reach the level of critical thinking skills. This has serious implications for the notion and practice of continuing professional development. The real concern here is that if students at undergraduate level demonstrate the use of strategic approaches to learning and choose to avoid engaging disjunction, then this can set a pattern for professional lives characterized by narrow frameworks and the inability to create and reframe knowledge for themselves. The result will be professionals who avoid engaging with issues and concepts that challenge their life-world in order that they can remain in comfortable frameworks and not allow themselves to be challenged nor to challenge the very frameworks in which they work.

In order to engage with these multiple agenda it is vital to acknowledge the complexity of managing professional territories and underlying attitudes and to do so in practical ways that enable students to understand the subtext of silent dialogues. One such way would to be to make explicit the actuality that knowledge is contingent, contextual and historical. This state of affairs needs to be recognized and then it will be possible to opt for the kind of knowledge in professional life characterized by transactional dialogue, critical self-reflection and responsiveness to change. It is only by embracing this kind of position that the shifting borders and the contextual nature of knowledge can be managed. This may then result in the kinds of professions that are self-learning communities and that help the development and continual renegotiation of professional frameworks and identities. However, it must also be acknowledged that these territories within professional education and practice are only to some extent maintained by the practising professionals themselves, the real culprits being the professional bodies who do not operate in the border countries where roles, purposes and identities are examined and multiply played out (Giroux, 1992). To live and work in the border countries is instead to position oneself at the edges of the language of universals and oppositions and to acknowledge the arbitrariness of boundaries and the changing condition of knowledge. There are some professional bodies who use the State or a Royal charter, or both, as a protection mechanism whenever they feel threatened by those nearby and with whose discipline boundaries they overlap. Few have realized (or are prepared to admit) that tradition is an illusion of permanence and that disciplines are unnatural categories. The result is that critical thought becomes almost impossible and that there is a rush to hide behind a kind of legitimated ideology where impassable barriers have been erected.

The consequence, which over time becomes devastating for the profession as a whole, is a merry band of experts who are knowledgeable only in narrowly defined parameters. In short:

> an army of alienated, privatized, and uncultured experts . . . This technical intelligentsia, rather than intellectuals in the traditional sense of thinkers concerned with the totality, is growing by leaps and bounds to run the increasingly complex bureaucratic and industrial apparatus. Its rationality, however, is only instrumental in character, and thus suitable mainly to perform partial tasks rather than tackling substantial questions of social organization and political direction.
>
> (Piccone, 1981–82: 16)

Professional bodies, which can engage with political issues, are needed to develop an understanding of professional life that acknowledges (and transcends) the boundaries that enable and disable it. Not only will they then be able to manage their own disjunctions, but they will also be able to embrace and critique a discourse of multiple possibilities for being. Students who are privileged to belong to a profession with a professional body that is able to manage radical practices will therefore be offered opportunities for developing critical choice.

Critical choice as a unifying framework?

Students may be offered opportunities for critical choice in learning but they may not understand what is on offer – or the relative costs of this kind of choice. Critical choice is seen here as opportunities for students to examine their learner stances and to explore the pedagogic influences on the development of their learner identity. However, it should be noted that, when faced with the expectation of understanding and managing these complex concepts, it is likely that many tutors would see their students running in the opposite direction. Yet within curricula students can be offered opportunities to explore frameworks in a whole variety of ways. On close inspection it is possible to see that students often only become aware of the possibility for critical choice through encountering disjunction and subsequent transition. Educators need to ensure that this process is enabling. It is vital that learning processes are not interrupted through such notions as what constitutes self-direction and student autonomy getting in the way. Griffiths (1992) has discussed the issues of autonomy and dependence and has suggested that the natures of both are badly misunderstood. Although this was spoken of in the context of schooling it has relevance here:

> Children dependent on the teacher's drawing up of their individual work programmes are said to have independent learning programmes.

Children who work in groups are said to be learning to be independent. Children who work by themselves in competition with each other are said to be learning to be independent. Children who, as a class, decide on topics and activities are said to be developing independence. Children working in a supportive group are in a good position to develop independence, but they are likely to be seduced by dependence into rejecting real learning and independent growth.

(Griffiths, 1992: 355)

This confusion about what might constitute autonomy and independence is also in evidence in post-school education, and possibly more so in professional education where issues of accountability to professional bodies affects what might constitute autonomy. Furthermore, there is a tendency to link autonomy with self-direction, which adds another confusion for the students. For example, students can become isolated in learning through self-direction and can experience disabling disjunction due to the expectation by students, tutor or both, that self-direction will be empowering when in fact for some it is not. Only an exploration of staff's own conceptions of autonomy and self-direction will enable them to explore the extent to which students can be enabled to make informed critical choices.

The image of the students at the beginning of the chapter captures the idea of critical choice in action. The occupational therapy student, having sifted through a variety of texts has, from her own stance, made decisions about what counts as valid knowledge. She can opt to have her views affirmed by university tutors, professionals in the field or her peers, in order to ensure that she has got the right end of the stick, intellectually speaking, but her intuition suggests to her that this may cause more problems than it solves. It is not just intuition, it is the realization that on the undergraduate programme she is undertaking she can only really discuss knowledge within given boundary conditions. Her options are to either subscribe to what is expected or attempt to push the boundaries by checking with the assessment tutor whether such boundary pushing is acceptable. Alternatively she can take a risk and submit a piece of work that she sees as valid from her stance as a learner. This is critical choice. It is a choice that involves personal risk in the light of understanding the hidden professional agenda and academic boundaries. Nevertheless it would seem that critical choices which students make often go unnoticed in higher education. Students' intentions in the learning process and their subsequent choices may not be articulated fully, or even at all. But when tutors deliberate about those whom they expected to do well on the programme, but who have underachieved, they may reflect that it is because of the choices that students have made. It is important for staff to realize that students' choices and intentions in learning, as well as what students see as legitimate issues at a personal, pedagogical and interactional level, are often the key to understanding their stances. Choice would also be central to the development of learner and professional identities.

Conclusion

Some of the struggles that students experience in the interaction of public theories, personal interpretations, academic boundaries and professional territories have been explored along with some of the difficulties in the relationship between outcome focused agenda and problem-based learning. The physicist whose notion of knowledge is based on a foundationalist view of learning where the assumption is that some knowledge is necessarily foundational to other knowledge, with content coverage being vital to most parts of the undergraduate programme, has, to some extent, been dealt with. The undergraduate student in occupational therapy is still somewhat left in a dilemma. Yet all these issues bring together the complex tapestry of higher education, which reflects to date perhaps less of the dominant culture of society and more the fragility and incoherence of the current age, where students are offered an *à la carte menu*.

Future educational reform from within higher education should therefore become increasingly concerned with the untold stories of the learners. There is a challenge to be taken up in the furthering of the dialogue of the relationship between conflicting experiences and ideological images, not just on the part of the learner but also on the part of all those involved in every component of academic life that affects the lives and identities of learners. The academe of recent years has had to learn to reinvent itself in numerous guises in relation to its customers and the government, and Barnett (1997b) has argued that the notion of teaching as a 'procedure' or the 'delivery of a body of knowledge' is no longer tenable. Modes of learning that interrupt linear models of learning, and which recognize the complexities of students' experience *can* offer students critical choice. They also become not just a theory of learning but also a practice whereby values and practices can be presented, explored and contested in the light of lived experience. In many curricula what is seen on the one hand are those students who opt out and sit on the edges and on the other those who buy into the belief that learning 'right answers' will mean getting a good degree. Yet most tutors know that those who do best for themselves are the ones who manage (strategically) the multiple agenda of higher education, professional education, practice contexts and personal ideals. These are the ones who have understood the subtext and made critical choices. To make such critical choices necessarily demands an understanding of the different levels of choice and an ability to critique these levels and their consequences. The subtext incorporates a whole host of interrelated issues that are discussed in the next chapter, where the kinds of problem-based learning curricula that are available are examined. It follows, therefore, that what is required is an understanding of the different forms of problem-based learning which might be on offer, not in any basic formulaic way, but in terms of the kinds of learning experiences that students are likely to have and the kinds of ways in which different issues may be played out pedagogically and professionally within these different models.

Part 4

Problem-based Learning
Reconsidered

9

Critical Perspectives on Problem-based Learning

Introduction

This chapter locates problem-based learning in the diverse world of higher education in general and begins by exploring, in brief, the ways in which interpretations of knowledge, learning and conceptions of the learner can affect the ways in which problem-based learning is played out in practice. The main body of the chapter presents five conceptual models of problem-based learning and examines the implications of utilizing each type. The chapter explores what is at stake when adopting one model of problem-based learning over another. Although each model is outlined in such a way as to imply, at one level, that they are to be seen as discrete, in fact the models do overlap to a large extent.

Between the ideas and the realities

Different forms of problem-based learning can offer staff and students opportunities for recognizing and valuing differences within the world of higher education. Problem-based learning would also seem to be a form of learning which can take account of, and challenge, the idea that there is a body of knowledge to be gained, a series of meanings to be understood and a number of techniques to be acquired. However, before these ideals are revisited it is necessary to understand first the focus of the debate. I argue here that what is required are forms of problem-based learning that not only offer students opportunities for critical contestability but also simultaneously offer them real choices about what and how to learn. Critical contestability is a position whereby students understand and acknowledge the transient nature of subject and discipline boundaries. They are able to transcend and interrogate these boundaries through a commitment to exploring the subtext of subjects and disciplines. Knowledge is thus contingent and contextual and as students interrogate the boundaries, the boundaries move continually in relation to one another. This will mean that a move is required beyond mere dialogue about the relationship between conflicting experiences and ideological images. Curricula are required that offer opportunities in learning that may enable students to realize *how* they construct their learner stances in relation to learner identity, learning context, peers, staff and past, present and future learning. This demands an understanding of the kinds of problem-based learning that embrace the notion of critical contestability and that bridge or fill the gaps between competing agenda. Problem-based learning for critical contestability will offer students opportunities to embrace, challenge or transcend the theories and practice put before them. Yet what might be the means by which students can be enabled and supported in the development of a learner identity that reflects the notion of critical contestability? In order to address this question the kinds of problem-based learning curricula on offer need to be examined, some of which go some way towards the ideal of critical contestability and others which offer little beyond instrumental reasoning.

Models and their modes

The form of problem-based learning in operation in curricula can largely be differentiated by the ways in which knowledge, learning and the role of the student are enacted within those curricula. This conceptualization may initially seem simplistic, but when the idea of staff's espoused theories and theories-in-use are examined, then what becomes apparent is that a complex, integrated course document, whilst often espousing the development of critique, does not often operate in a way conducive to such development. Although much has been written about knowledge, which challenges existing concepts, from forms of knowledge, through critical theory, to the post modern movement, it is in fact staff's pedagogical stances that will reflect what is seen as valid knowledge by students. Thus, the positioning of knowledge in a problem-based learning programme will tell us more about the pedagogical stances of the staff than the forms of knowledge in action. Learning will be defined almost inevitably by the ways in which problems are expected to be solved or managed as well as through the assessment process. In practice, therefore, this might mean that within the same curriculum any number of models could be in operation. For example, the facilitator's influence on the group may mean that the focus is on epistemological competence. Here the facilitator sees himself as a guide to knowledge acquisition and problem solution with the result that students will experience all that goes with Model I: Problem-based learning for epistemological competence. Meanwhile in the adjacent seminar room a different problem-based learning group has a facilitator whose focus is on equipping students with skills for the work place. She sees her role as one of demonstrating excellence in practice and therefore her students experience Model II: Problem-based learning for professional action.

The way in which students are perceived by staff, and what is meant by being a student will also have an effect. For if students are not encouraged to value their prior learning, to value their own perspectives or to challenge the frameworks from the world of work then the possibility for critical contestability will be diminished. Problem-based programmes, both in theory and in practice, have largely emerged through the personal and pedagogical stances of the faculty members involved in the development and facilitation of those programmes. Yet it must be acknowledged too that these models and their modes are not only affected by the ways in which tutors position themselves in relation to the learner, but also the positions that the students take up in response to the tutors. Students will 'read' a tutor in a particular way and these interpretations will affect the student's understanding of what is seen as learning, the way knowledge is to be interpreted and in some cases their notion of what it means to be a professional. For example, engineering lecturers are those who also embody, to a greater or lesser extent, what it means to be an engineer. Ways of problem-based learning are required that help students to not only examine their learner stances but also construct a view about what is being presented to them. Salmon has argued: 'I do not think we have gone very far in understanding how it is that individual learners actually come to construct their own unique material. This may be because the material of learning has traditionally been viewed in different terms from those that define the learner. To do so may mean thinking very differently about the whole question of learning' (Salmon, 1989: 231). The following series of models (see Table 9.1) is offered as a means of understanding ways in which learners are enabled and disabled in the process of constructing knowledge for themselves, depending on the form of problem-based learning with which they are faced.

Model I Problem-based learning for epistemological competence

Model I is characterized by a view of knowledge that is essentially propositional, with students being expected to become competent in applying knowledge in the context of solving, and possibly managing, problems. Those wedded to a concept of knowledge of this sort would be unlikely to debunk the myths connected with this view of knowledge since in Model I what counts as valid knowledge is defined in advance and all other viewpoints are largely ruled out. Students are expected, therefore, to know how to use propositional knowledge to solve given problems. Thus, knowledge is seen as being certain and the solutions to the problems are already known by the staff and known to be specific by the students. Problem-based learning is therefore used as a means of helping students to learn content. As such, problem situations are seen as the means by which students become competent in knowledge management and in covering the required content in the curriculum.

Table 9.1   Models of problem-based learning

	Model I *PBL for Epistemological Competence*	Model II *PBL for Professional Action*
Knowledge	Propositional	Practical and performative
Learning	The use and management of a propositional body of knowledge to solve or manage a problem	The outcome-focused acquisition of knowledge and skills for the work place
Problem scenario	Limited – solutions already known and are designed to promote cognitive understanding	Focused on a real-life situation that requires an effective practical resolution
Students	Receivers of knowledge who acquire and understand propositional knowledge through problem-solving	Pragmatists inducted into professional cultures who can undertake practical action
Facilitator	A guide to obtaining the solution and to understanding the correct propositional knowledge	A demonstrator of skills and a guide to 'best practice'
Assessment	The testing of a body of knowledge to ensure students have developed epistemological competence	The testing of skills and competencies for the work place supported by a body of knowledge

In practice, problem-based learning will largely be based within a particular discipline area, such as economics or engineering, and the problem scenarios will be based on key concepts about which students are expected to know. Model I has many of the components of problem-solving learning. What is different in Model I is that problem-based learning is also being used to enable students to develop problem-solving abilities, to become competent in applying their knowledge to solve problems and, in parallel with professional practice, to test students' understanding of what has been taught. Thus, there may be conflicts within the problem-based learning programme. This may occur between those tutors who expect students to adopt a step-by-step model to solving problems in order to 'cover ground'

Model III *PBL for Interdisciplinary* *Understanding*	*Model IV* *PBL for Transdisciplinary* *Learning*	*Model V* *PBL for Critical* *Contestability*
Propositional, performative and practical	The examining and testing out of given knowledge and frameworks	Contingent, contextual and constructed
The synthesis of knowledge with skills across discipline boundaries	Critical thought and decentring oneself from disciplines in order to understand them	A flexible entity that involves interrogation of frameworks
Acquiring knowledge to be able to do, therefore centred around knowledge with action	Characterized by resolving and managing dilemmas	Multidimensional, offering students options for alternative ways of knowing and being
Integrators across boundaries	Independent thinkers who take up a critical stance towards learning	Explorers of underlying structures and belief systems
A coordinator of knowledge and skill acquisition across boundaries of both	An orchestrator of opportunities for learning (in its widest sense)	A commentator, a challenger and decoder of cultures, disciplines and traditions
The examination of skills and knowledge in a context that may have been learned out of context	The opportunity to demonstrate an integrated understanding of skills and personal and propositional knowledge across disciplines	Open-ended and flexible

and gain depth and rigour in basic sciences, and those tutors who are expecting students to use a more creative approach for gaining the answer. Learning in this model will be seen as the process of acquiring the right knowledge to solve the problem and offering an answer that fits broadly with a tutor's preset agenda. It will be largely devoid of visceral experiences of learning or the use of learners' own autobiographical material, unless of course it provides some useful facts and guidance that facilitates the arrival at the correct solution. However, learner experience will be seen by the problem-based learning group as secondary to lecturers' perspectives or articles and textbooks written by experts. For the student, learning is about the process of attaining the correct answer and of developing enough understanding of the propositional knowledge to be able to solve the problem. Content will be perceived by them as 'out there' and independent of themselves as learners. Students will therefore see themselves as capable of receiving, reproducing and researching knowledge supplied by experts and using problem-based learning to develop their understanding of the relationship between the knowledge and its practical application.

Students will be viewed as receivers of knowledge and they will be expected to manage any disjunction they experience by themselves. Difficulties encountered within the groups will be disregarded by the tutors who will expect them to sort out any problematic issues themselves. The tutor, as facilitator, is there to guide students towards the right answer or the means of managing the situation effectively. Within this model student approaches to learning tend to be characterized by reproductive pedagogy, exemplified by students assimilating and reproducing information supplied by academics, on academics' terms, and strategic pedagogy, typified by students buying into the academics' agenda and dominant perspectives and adapting their learning to that which they perceive is expected of them. Thus, students will adopt approaches to enable them to pass the course by the best means available to them. This in turn may mean that students in this model also adopt an individualistic position towards the group, either because disabling disjunction resulted in a sense of fragmentation in their personal stance, which meant that working in isolation was less threatening than admitting failure to peers, or because it was seen as a means of gaining a better qualification than other group members. Alternatively, students struggling to make sense of propositional knowledge may have an enabling effect by helping other group members to begin to legitimize their own knowledge and to move to a position of 'validated knowing'. Students are helped by peers to value and utilize prior experiences, to develop confidence and to renew their learning aspirations.

Model II Problem-based learning for professional action

This model of problem-based learning has, as its overarching concept, the notion of 'know-how'. Action is seen here as the defining principle of the curriculum whereby learning is both around what it will enable students to do, and around mechanisms that are perceived to enable students to become competent to practice. Through this process of problem-based learning, students learn how to problem solve and to become competent in applying this ability to other kinds of problem scenarios and situations within given frameworks. So the students develop critical thinking skills for the work place, interpreted somewhat narrowly as the ability to use problem-solving abilities in relation to propositional knowledge as a means of becoming competent in the work place and being able to turn on these skills at any given point.

This kind of model is seen, and has to a large extent emerged from, those curricula that have strong links with public and private industry and which are largely influenced by the world of work such as business studies, social work and occupational therapy. Undergraduate courses such as surveying and law are less influenced by this focus of learning for professional action, since the undergraduate programme is required to place its emphasis on propositional knowledge, which is then followed by a postgraduate training and qualification period. The limit of this model is its tendency to focus on skills acquisition in the context of the university with the somewhat mistaken assumption that these can necessarily be transferred to the world of work (Bridges, 1993; Havard *et al.*, 1998). Students are expected to do the transferring but few tutors, it seems, tell them how to do this. The idea of transferring skills seems to have resulted from a desire to enable students to become more equipped to cope with complex and unstructured situations. Skills, such as teamwork, communication, presentation and problem-solving are high profile and good money spinners in higher education – reflecting some of the more recent political shifts, at government level, to all style and no content. However, the very notion of equipping students with particular skills and competencies to manage complexities, downgrades the understanding of what it means to be a professional, and offers the students instead a notion of the professional as someone who has a tool kit of skills to apply to any situation.

So the question in this kind of problem-based learning is not what counts as knowledge, but what are legitimate skills to transfer and how can the transference of meta-skills be enabled? It will be important in these kinds of curricula to ensure that skills-based learning does not become a form of behavioural training in which competence to practise can be ticked off against a check list. An example of this can be seen in the kinds of oversimplistic training methods used in some clinical skills laboratories, where skills learning is isolated from the context in which the ability is to be used. In curricula such as this, everything is seen in terms of its use value and little opportunity will be offered for the development of deep level understanding, professional judgement or personal meaning. The danger therefore, with Model II, is that problem-based learning is being used as a mechanism to develop narrow sets of skills that may feel to the students somewhat divorced from any other forms of knowledge. For example, an overemphasis on communication skills or teamwork, without students being encouraged to engage with and reflect on the related theory and current research, can result in uncritical acceptance of the guidance given by tutors. Furthermore, skills taught without the backing of theory and research will not help students to consider the possibility that different kinds of team work skills may be needed in the workplace, compared with those that they have been encouraged to develop at university. Skills and know-how are not to be thrown out, but what will be needed in this kind of problem-based learning are concepts of skills and know-how firmly rooted in the notion of skills *with* cognitive content and professional judgement.

Model III Problem-based learning for interdisciplinary understanding

In this model of problem-based learning there is a shift away from a demand for mere know-how and propositional knowledge. Instead, problem-based learning becomes a vehicle to bridge the gap between the know-how and know-that and between the different forms of disciplinary knowledge in the curriculum. In practice what occurs is an attempt by staff to develop in their students a form of understanding that is interdisciplinary, both across forms of propositional knowledge and in the sense of using meta-skills across the boundaries of the world of work and the academic context.

Barnett (1994) has argued that interdisciplinarity is no longer possible, in fact that it is dead, because its axioms in use are being undermined. But the argument is more complex than deciding that interdisciplinarity is dead. Disciplines are growing stronger in striving to maintain their boundaries – and in an attempt to retain their staff in the face of cutbacks. This is occurring to such an extent that curricula are becoming fragmented through the wholehearted, and often inappropriate, imposition of disciplinary frameworks by university decision makers on curricula that are educating students for the professions that take their roots from a number of subject areas and disciplines. Let us take, for example, a degree in nursing. A group of staff implement problem-based learning to promote interdisciplinary understanding. Staff's intentions are that students will be able to make sense of components of knowledge that overlap across subject areas and disciplines and integrate the knowledge, which they have acquired as individuals, into the group learning process. Thus, the focus of problem-based learning will be on the students being able to understand and synthesize information rather than to have to gain a particular depth of coverage. Staff want students to be able to know about, for example, physiology, the psychology of learning and how to use a particular computer package. They also require students to know how to use this knowledge in the practice situation. To these staff problem-based learning seems to be an ideal means of equipping the students to do both.

Meanwhile, back in the university's executive offices, negotiations have been underway between the Nursing college and the university and it has been decided to merge an existing local nursing programme into the university. Later, cascaded decision making, with an eye on financial savings, has led to staff from the physiology and psychology departments teaching their specific disciplines on the nursing degree. It matters not that the nursing tutors (with degrees in physiology, psychology and nursing) possess ten years' experience in delivering their curriculum in a way that promotes interdisciplinary understanding. Thus, curricula become disabled by imposed disciplinary boundaries, and fragmented learning experiences result for students, because lecturers from other disciplines cannot help them to make the links between the physiology of the kidney and prolonged bed rest. What is more, the focus by other disciplines upon propositional knowledge will mean that students are merely supplied with chunks of knowledge in isolation. Students discovering that same knowledge for themselves from problem-based scenarios are likely to find it far more relevant and memorable.

In Model III the student works, learns and develops herself *within* subjects and disciplines. She understands that disciplines taught as discrete entities do overlap, but that she must make the necessary connections for herself. The connections she makes are in the relationships *between* the disciplines. Learning is therefore seen here as knowing and understanding knowledge from the disciplines, and also recognizing the relationship between them, so making sense for herself both personally and pedagogically. This kind of problem-based learning unites disciplines with skills (of all sorts), such that the student is able to see, from her stance as a future professional, the relationship between her personal stance and the propositional knowledge of the disciplines. She is enabled to develop not only an epistemological position but also a practice-related perspective that integrates knowing-that with knowing-how.

Model IV Problem-based learning for transdisciplinary learning

In this model problem-based learning operates in a way that enables the students to recognize that disciplinary boundaries exist but that they are also somewhat illusory, that they have been erected. The student might transcend boundaries but he is not likely to challenge the frameworks into which disciplinary knowledge is placed. According to Popper (1970), all thought (and presumably action and experience), takes place within some kind of framework, although we are not forever confined to this framework. Barnett (1994) has argued that Popper avoided the issue that the practical rules of a particular framework forbid an examination of that framework. To do so would run counter to the very nature of the framework, because by deconstructing one framework that is the basis of the discipline, other related frameworks thereby become problematic as all the other connecting boundaries become problematic. In Model IV, the frameworks are not reframed (as in Model V) since to do that would risk jettisoning those frameworks. Instead, what occurs in practice is that knowledge and skills are 'kept in their place' and that students have an overview of the frameworks, which does not risk disturbing them.

Students in this model tend to adopt such stances as pedagogical autonomy, a position of learning that they perceive will offer them the greatest degree of autonomy. For these students learning does not have to fit entirely within the remit of that defined by authorities, and thus students are independent in making decisions about how they learn. Learning here, therefore, involves utilizing critical thought to decentre one's self from disciplines in order to transcend them. Here, decentring (Habermas, 1990) is not seen in the Habermasian sense of a *radical* transcendence of one's prior beliefs, personal needs and social norms, but in terms of a reflection on, and an openness towards, the stances of others and, therefore, necessarily an evaluation of one's own. It is also about integrating what one knows tacitly with what else is on offer and as a result integrating and transcending boundaries simultaneously. Students are therefore encouraged to integrate learning into their deepest level of understanding and consequently to integrate theory and practice across discipline boundaries, knowing that the boundaries are somewhat arbitrary. For example, students will see that the notion of caring for clients requires them to both take up a position on their concept of care and understand those same theories of care as transcending the disciplines of, for example, psychiatry and physical medicine. Yet this will only be a relativistic attitude and they will see that theories are not truth but metaphors with which to interpret data (Perry, 1970).

In this model of problem-based learning, students are encouraged to adopt a critical position towards knowledges, themselves and their peers, and to use the problem-based learning group as a place in which to examine and test out personal and pedagogical frameworks. Students here will tend to develop a highly autonomous position as individuals within a group, and as a group. They will elect to use the group to resolve dilemmas and to discover meaning in their lives, to the extent that the facilitator becomes an orchestrator of opportunities. The danger with this model, however, is that the facilitators see students as such autonomous learners that they opt out of facilitating the group that is moving towards a position of criticality. This reduces facilitation to a skills-based task that focuses purely on process and ignores the quality of what students actually produce and feed back to the group. Thus, instead of the students integrating knowledge and skills across the boundaries, by, as it were, filling the gaps between disciplines for themselves, as in Model III, here they take a position of being critical thinkers; autonomous learners who use discipline boundaries to make sense of multiple ways of knowing. Students working within this model will see value in discipline boundaries being something against which to take up a critical stance. However, transcendence of the boundaries will not mean an interrogation of the disciplines, but rather the adoption of a position towards what is on offer.

Model V Problem-based learning for critical contestability

The implementation of problem-based learning in many professional and disciplinary areas has occurred because of the increasing need to find ways to help students to develop the capacity to manage their own learning in the face of modularization, technological learning and a decrease in the unit of resource. For many staff though, it has also emerged from a desire to foster in students a kind of critical thought that can be used to promote insight into multidimensional problems. The realization that this kind of thought is dependent, not only on the integration of know-that with know-how, but also on the contextual nature of the situation(s) in which the problem has arisen, has led many to aspire to the kind of problem-based learning seen in Model V.

This form of problem-based learning is one that seeks to provide for the students a kind of higher education which offers, within the curriculum, multiple models of action, knowledge, reasoning and reflection, along with opportunities for the students to challenge, evaluate and interrogate them. Students will therefore examine the underlying structures and belief systems implicit within a discipline or profession itself, in order to not only understand the disciplinary area but also its credence. They will transcend and interrogate disciplinary boundaries through a commitment to exploring the subtext of those disciplines. Thus, students are encouraged to challenge borders, create new borders, live and work in the border country and, at the same time, begin to know how to live in that country (Giroux, 1992). Knowledge here is seen as being constructed by the students, who begin to see themselves as creators of knowledge, and who become able to build on and integrate previously learned knowledge and skills with material that is currently being learned. Students are encouraged to evaluate critically both personal knowledge and propositional knowledge on their own terms; thus the student embraces knowledge and also queries it.

Therefore, in the context of their peer group, students are encouraged to make knowledge claims that are put before the group for examination by others in order to facilitate shifts not just towards critical contestability but also ideally towards the acquisition of a critical spirit (Barnett, 1997a), through which students can evaluate themselves, the world and knowledge in relation to one another. Individuals will use dialogue and argument as an organizing principle in life so that through dialogue they will challenge assumptions, make decisions and rethink goals. Students will use the group process to challenge identity and all that is implicit within that identity. Thus, students are expected to develop qualities of moral and intellectual, as well as emotional, independence. In addition, they are required to set their own goals and delineate their own processes for learning. Within the problem-based programme they are offered opportunities to examine themselves as reflexive projects and to discover and to develop their own voices, so experiencing a continual state of personal and pedagogical renewal.

As future practitioners it is intended that students would be enabled to become questioning and critical practitioners; practitioners who would not only evaluate themselves and their peers effectively, but would also be able to analyse the shortcomings of policy and practice. Students involved in this form of problem-based learning would tend to adopt reflective pedagogy. They will see learning and epistemology as flexible entities, perceive that there are also other valid ways of seeing things besides their own perspective, and accept that all kinds of knowing can help them to know the world and themselves more effectively.

Problem-based learning of this sort enables students to develop a critical position from which to interpret the practice of others, to (re)develop their own critical perspectives and thence to critique them. Here, students' personal, pedagogical and interactional stances are acknowledged and valued (as well as challenged) within the curriculum, with disjunction being seen as a central principle. What this means is that disjunction will be seen as an essential concept in the curriculum through which students are encouraged to learn to manage uncertainty for themselves and as a means of being and becoming reflexive projects.

The difficulties with this model largely stem from issues of power and control in the learning context. Staff's sense of self is likely to feel at risk or threatened in their role in the group and in relation to their conceptions of learning and knowledge, since they will be under increasing scrutiny from the students. It might be that the enactment of this model is only actually possible in the context of postgraduate programmes, where students are offered more freedom to learn in the context of their own agenda than in undergraduate or pre-registration (professional) curricula.

Conclusion

It is only the final model, Model V, that can provide a form of problem-based learning which offers students opportunities to move towards critical contestability. Some of the other models may equip students to make transitions in some domains of their learner stances that will prompt a shift towards critical contestability. Yet it should be noted that critical contestability is not seen as the ultimate sphere to be attained, rather it is seen as a place from which one can then make critical choices about further decisions, such as whether to adopt a different domain within one's personal, pedagogical or interactional stance. However, it might be argued here that, with the increasing shifts towards accountability and professional and academic competence characterized by the performative slide, in reality Model V is just a Utopian dream, an ideal that cannot be realized, or an exception in terms of individual students, particular cohorts of students or students from well-funded institutions.

10

Problem-based Learning and Organizational Cultures

Introduction

There is a sense, in the unstable state of higher education, that the continual renegotiation of frameworks, structures and ideals means that we are, in a sense, always in crisis. Reflexive modernization, the process by which the classical industrial society has modernized itself, has resulted in a sense of crisis characterized by a 'risk society' (Beck, 1992). This type of society with its emerging themes of ecological safety, the danger of losing control over scientific and technological innovations and the growth of a more flexible labour force will have a profound effect upon higher education. Jansen and Van Der Veen (1992: 276) have argued:

> The study and practice of adult education cannot afford to ignore these themes, if adult education pretends to contribute to solutions for actual social problems. The most fascinating question for adult education is how these new themes will be translated into new methods. Will these methods shed new light, for example, on the integration of instrumental, expressive and sociological learning, on experiential learning and on mutual directivity between facilitator and participant?

Ways of managing this fragmenting culture might be seen not just as living with risk but as living in the borders, not moving towards the end of higher education or the end of the university, but along the brink, along the edges of the end. This chapter therefore focuses on an examination of the interrelationship between problem-based learning and the complex, interconnected, institutional problems that occur at the interface of structures and people in the context of innovation. It explores the ways in which organizations, and management systems within them, can move towards, and manage, the tensions relating to a kind of problem-based learning that will embrace and engage with the complex terrain of higher education in such a turbulent environment. The chapter begins, however, with a review of the relationship between the framework of Dimensions of Learner Experience and the wider political and organizational issues in higher education.

Retrospect and prospect

Dimensions of Learner Experience may be used as a framework for making sense of problem-based learning. Simultaneously, it may be used as a framework to demonstrate ways in which problem-based learning may prompt, for some students, a de/reconstruction of taken-for-granted realities that ultimately enables them to give meaning to the realities of their past, present and future learning; meaning that may not have arisen through more traditional methods of teaching. Yet to decontextualise problem-based learning from organizational change, issues of innovation and change, and political agenda, can result in formulaic practices that deny, as it were, the very quiddity of life: 'just as the essence of food cannot be expressed in terms of calories, so the essence of life is not to be conveyed by a formula, however brilliant' (Solzhenitsyn, 1988: 348). In terms of the literature and research into problem-based learning – including my own – a number of challenges emerge that must be set in context. For example, by embarking on an exploration of student and staff experiences of problem-based learning it is often assumed that it will be possible to locate and make sense of the complexities inherent in this approach to learning. The worldwide literature on problem-based learning discusses definitions, practices, evaluations of problem-based learning and a whole host of other issues whilst also raising the importance of using prior experience for learning. The difficulty and complexity of attempting to explore staff's and students' experiences means that issues of context, prior experience and learner history tend to slip in and out of focus. In-depth explorations of problem-based learning as a concept or way of learning invariably result in collisions with matters connected with people's lives in complex changing institutions characterized by a range of teaching and learning strategies. Students and staff with whom I spoke could not separate their experience of problem-based learning from how they talked about themselves and their learner identity, and their personal, pedagogical and interactional concerns. Vernon and Blake have captured the essence of the dilemma encountered when examining and researching problem-based learning (although in a slightly positivist vein):

> Conducting a high-quality evaluative research on problem-based learning has been difficult for a variety of reasons. The more independent variable, problem-based learning, is more than a simple teaching method. It is better described as a complex mixture of a general teaching philosophy, learning objectives and goals, and faculty attitudes and values, all of which are difficult to regulate and are often not very well defined in research reports. The outcome variables that are often most

highly valued, and best exemplify the special features of problem-based learning are often complex, multidimensional and difficult to measure.
(Vernon and Blake, 1993: 560)

Thus, Dimensions of Learner Experience and the notion of the three stances offer one way of understanding how construction and deconstruction of learner experience mediates between a host of internal and external factors that impact upon staff's and students' lives. Yet there is still a certain sense in which problem-based learning can be talked about in isolation from other issues: this in the context of both the dearth of literature about students' experiences of problem-based learning and the organizational impact of implementing problem-based learning.

Inside and outside organizations

This section revisits some of the issues that were discussed in Chapter 1 but also explores new issues that have emerged recently (Savin-Baden, 1998) in the light of current trends and changes in higher education. So often it seems that texts end with ease and a sense of a conclusion. This is not so here. Instead, there are chasms that have yet to be fully explored in the changing terrain of problem-based learning, set in the often somewhat grinding organization of the UK higher education system. Problem-based learning operates within an organization, but also stretches over the boundaries of other organizations. In particular, it sits at the interface of industry (public and private sector) and higher education. Thus, those utilizing problem-based learning for critical contestability must learn to live life in the border country; an area where learner identities can be explored and (re)constructed and learning contexts can be refashioned to allow for the 'opening up of communicative spaces' (Niemi and Kemmis, 1999), spaces where networks of communication can be identified and created and in which critical contestability can emerge.

Yet, at the same time, problem-based learning can interrupt and disable the organizational culture as well as be disrupted by it. For example, problem-based learning can prompt 'creative destruction' (Schumpeter, 1934) in an organization whereby the innovation challenges and destroys established practice. New innovations are intended to displace old innovations. This, in turn, is expected to create a pattern whereby new solutions are generated through the solving (or managing) of problems. This may be the case in many organizations, but difficulty arises when innovations such as problem-based learning are bolted onto courses but are believed by some staff to be a new innovation. Other staff may ignore its very existence, or argue that they 'have been doing problem-based learning for years', even if their conceptions of problem-based learning differ markedly from other broad interpretations of its use. The consequence is that problem-based learning will not displace the old innovation but will become displaced by the old, as it comes adrift amidst seats of power and competing staff agenda.

One of the central difficulties with universities is that, as organizations, they nowadays tend to adopt strategies focused upon solving problems. The epitome of this could be said to be in the Dearing Report's (NCIHE, 1997) emphasis on predominantly operational solutions (see for example Weil, 1999). Furthermore, in recent years, the shifts in the structure of universities worldwide have been designed to emulate business organizations, as seen in the adoption of an enterprise culture. What is emerging is an image of a competent university manager as one who is able to solve the technical problems encountered by blue chip universities. Therefore, at the top there is an executive team characterized by ideologies that concentrate on the application of private sector management values and practices, such as customer care, outcome measures, benchmarking and performance-related pay. Under this can be found layers of lecturers who are unlikely to be attuned or even prepared to engage with this culture; instead they maintain a collegial or bureaucratic structure, depending on what supports their purposes, and reinforce the bunkers around their disciplines. Meanwhile students are being encouraged, through approaches such as problem-based learning, to manage complexity and challenge frameworks. Simultaneously, UK government attention to detail in the areas of teaching and research quality and standards is expected to improve the overall efficiency and effectiveness of the university as an organization without disturbing the sense of it as a culture of a 'loosely coupled system' (Weick, 1988).

Political issues with organizational and educational implications

Government policy on higher education has had an increasing impact worldwide. During the period 1988–1991, the Australian higher education system shifted from an élite to a mass system (the UK doing so in the 1980s) and this was more managerial and bureaucratic than in former years (Taylor *et al.*, 1998). The issue of teaching performance has been addressed through mechanisms such as setting up staff development units, examining teaching quality and granting university prizes for effective teaching. Such trends have emerged in other countries and are now also a feature of the UK system. The supply of funding for different initiatives has brought about a perspective that government intervention in higher education can put important agenda, such as access and student learning quality, centre stage. Alternatively, government intervention can also distort higher education practices, for example through the influence, in the UK, of such activities as the Research Assessment Exercise (RAE). However, problem-based learning can offer managers (and executives), staff and students, a means of living with organizational dilemmas. The very disjunction that ensues from these challenges can enable those involved in problem-based learning, at whatever level, to hold and manage incompatibilities. Problem-based learning *can* encourage managers to hold in tension two seemingly opposing choices rather than necessarily having to choose between them.

Organizational issues to be considered by those wishing to implement problem-based learning, and perhaps by those wishing to evaluate current problem-based learning curricula are as follows:

- The declining unit of resource in higher education will impact on the student experience in terms of fewer resources (rooms in which to meet, and study and library materials) and staff time available for students. Staff who are on short-term contracts or who are brought in for short periods of time are less inclined to help students when they are only paid to teach and not necessarily to facilitate learning. A further concern is that interprofessional education is being seen by some staff and university executives as means of teaching more students with less resources, and problem-based learning is being increasingly viewed as a vehicle for its implementation.
- The shift to mass higher education can offer variety and choice for those who have previously had little or no access to the system. At the same time it also offers greater diversity for students about when and how they learn, in a culture where the level and availability of grants and loans mean that many study from home. The idea that students migrate to engage with a kind of liberal education that equips them for life, as well as to be taught within a discipline, is available to few. Part-time higher education is much more likely to be the future. This may also mean an increase in degree completion time, because students can perhaps only afford to undertake one module per year. As a result, full-time under-graduate learning, which includes the types of opportunities that pro-mote learning with and through others, such as problem-based learning, may only become an option for the affluent or for those universities who can manage to develop learning communities across cyber space.
- In the UK the impact of the Research Assessment Exercise on teaching and learning is encouraging élitism in research to the extent that some staff are put aside to undertake research to ensure continuing high attainment. Taylor *et al.* (1998) have argued that, despite recent govern-ment initiatives in Australia, respondents in their study believed that the under-valuing of teaching compared with research continued to persist in higher education. Staff (rather than students) may also be 'dumbed down' (Simon, 1996) to teaching, or even become part of a strategic move to shift them, as a department, into another university that has more of a teaching focus, because they are too much of a risk to be part of the RAE. There seems to be a fissure appearing between teaching and research. The same proportions of staff in both the old and the new universities believe that teaching has become less important in their discipline gener-ally (Harley and Lowe, 1998). Despite the Dearing Report and the crea-tion of the Institute of Learning and Teaching, it is likely that alternative opportunities for knowledge creation that promote learning for critical

contestability will become marginalized by political motivations to gain research monies and status at the expense of teaching. Yet the key problem with the RAE is that:

> management discourse may indeed have found it hard to penetrate the walls of academe, management practice has not . . . the RAE is such an effective mechanism of management control precisely because it does not *need* to replace one type of discourse with another. In co-opting peer review for managerial ends, the RAE offers individuals the possibility of securing material and symbolic rewards without ostensible violence to the traditional value systems which constitute academic identity.
>
> (Harley and Lowe, 1998)

Thus, problem-based learning, which is a form of learning that puts research and evaluation at its core, stands to be excluded from universities that do just that. This is because it is a method that demands much of its staff in their role as facilitators; yet it is these very skills and abilities for which staff will receive little kudos at the élite (research-led) end of the university sector.

- Student diversity is increasing and higher education of the future will have a significant number of mature students. This is particularly pertinent as the percentage of mature and part-time students has increased compared with full-time and younger students (AUT, 1995). It is also likely that there will be an increased gender shift. Currently UK and USA schoolgirls are performing better than boys, and this may mean that the higher education of the future will need to recognize women's requirements in order to both attract and retain them. Yet, although higher education at one level would appear to be more accessible (in the shift to a mass system), there seems to be little change in the ways in which, overall, the institutions have adapted their processes to meet the needs of the new customers in the system. Seemingly there is not even a recognition by higher education institutions that a cultural change is required to address these shifts in an attempt to match the needs of a growing and diverse student population.
- The impact of the Institute of Learning and Teaching (ILT) in the UK is something that is viewed by many with a degree of scepticism. The Institute of Learning and Teaching is a virtual institution formed as a result of recommendations by the Dearing Report into Higher Education (NCIHE, 1997). The idea is that this institution will accredit programmes, which have been set up to train and establish lecturers' teaching effectiveness, to enhance research and development into teaching and learning, and to stimulate innovation in teaching and learning. There are those who feel that whilst it may be something that is required in the higher education of the future, the current low status of teaching in general along with the token funding the ILT has received means that it will have little lasting impact on the face of higher education. There already seem to be confusions

in the messages being proffered by those involved, in terms of structures and mechanisms, who act as if it were possible or even desirable to create and perpetuate a stable state. This is particularly apparent in relation to notions of accountability and improvement. As Weil has so aptly pointed out: 'The Dearing Report stresses the management of change in HE through structures that increase systematic control. It does not emphasize the need for structures and incentive/reward processes that support continuous systematic learning and inquiry in action or transdisciplinary innovation and responsiveness' (Weil, 1999: 184). Although the ILT has been severely criticized there are important opportunities to be gained by the alliance of those who have already proven experience in this field (for example the Staff and Educational Development Association (SEDA). Such alliances may also be a step towards raising the status of teaching in the UK and elsewhere. However, better equipped and enabled teachers in higher education will not necessarily mean that they have an impact on the culture of their institutions or on the kinds of learning and re- search that are and are not rewarded. It might mean though that they are able to equip students to learn effectively and to decide from the myriad of learning experiences and technologies on offer what might challenge and best equip them to be critical learners and workers for the future.

- 'Talking Heads' used to demonstrate exemplary practice is being mooted as a way forward to help to improve teaching practices. The idea is to video 'so-called' experts in teaching (Talking Heads) who exhibit flawless practice so that others may mimic this behaviour across the UK. Yet this seems to be an attempt to move back to apprentice-style methods. The whole idea of exemplary practice brings with it the notions of a 'right way' to do things, rather than any kind of real notion of Talking Heads *à la* Bennett (Bennett, 1988), has who offered diverse perspectives on life through the previously untold stories of people's lives. It seems odd that, while the Dearing Report has argued for more effective and innovative teaching, there continue to be such suggestions as Talking Heads and a rise in 'How to' guides and seminars that deny any sense of critique or analysis of the proffered frameworks. Instead, these guides present a rational world in which tasks are to be achieved by mastering the necessary skills and abilities, and thus any real sense that to be a lecturer in higher education encompasses multiple ways of knowing and being is denied.

Organizational structures that impinge upon problem-based learning

Within most organizations there exists a variety of cultures that are evident in the differing practices and this is no less the case in higher education. It would seem that within the scope of the complex layers of these unwieldy institutions there are often organizational cultures that stand at polar oppos- ites. This may be why the university has managed to sustain itself over such a period of time, it might also be the reason why the borders around it are currently on the move. Matters of organizational structure and culture incorporate concerns about management styles and notions of leadership, curriculum design and departmental structures. One of the interesting omissions in the problem-based learning literature is that of the relationship between the organizational structures and the 'fit' of problem-based learning within that culture, as well as the fit with the discipline into which the problem-based learning is to be placed. Problem-based learning as both an innovation and an approach to learning can affect, and be affected by, any or all of the following issues.

Organizational structure and culture can affect the way in which problem-based learning is implemented and enacted, particularly since the broad shift from collegial models of higher education to those of enterprise styles has occurred (McNay, 1995). For example, the shift to enterprise cultures has brought with it closer links between industry and higher education and the 'good of the client' is now seen as paramount. Accountability, competencies and professionalism are all features of this culture, but it is also a culture that can bring a loss of educational coherence through an over dominance of market related values in curricula. Mixtures of cultures and structures adopted across one institution can also result in problems of fit between institutional research policies centred around a collegial system, and the flexibility required at the same time for the university to compete in the market-place. Add into this the adoption of a matrix structure and there is the following scenario. The university has adopted an enterprise culture overall and is seeking to sustain this through a view of leadership that is seen as a group function within a changing organization, and therefore leadership is seen to take on a number of different forms. At departmental level there is a head of department who sees himself as a chief executive, who espouses corporate values and who has adopted a matrix structure in order to encourage innovative and adaptive behaviour in the staff. This means that a large and often fragmented department, such as medicine, can be team driven and transcend subject specialism, such as haematology, psychology and orthopaedics. Yet the needs of those within the specialism destroy the team culture because in fact the department is bureaucratic in nature and therefore the matrix structure does not work. Instead, the department is undermined through conflicts between subject and team loyalties. This results in teams failing to undertake their roles effectively because they find it too difficult to break free of their subject driven loyalties. In such a situation problem-based learning can become the scapegoat for wider organizational concerns, or collapse during implementation because it was a team remit subsequently destroyed by subject-based agenda.

Management in higher education is rapidly becoming seen as a means to replace scarce resources and to provide organizational solutions to something that in many ways could be seen as an economic and social problem. For example, staff who were interviewed (Savin-Baden, 1996) reported that the business ethic of the university was affecting the overall quality of the courses on offer, and that this was worsened by the institutional emphasis on procuring funds and research monies rather than valuing quality learning. At the same time, the shift to teaching larger student numbers and with it the management decision to build larger and larger lecture theatres has meant that there is less (if any) space for small group teaching, and little overall flexibility for courses that have adopted alternative teaching and learning methods to lecturing. However, what appears to be coming to the fore is the importance and value of leadership in higher education (Middlehurst, 1995). This seems to be because of the sheer magnitude of change occurring in higher education that is prompting a view that leadership can help the organization to develop a broader range of strategies for change than in former years. As a result, leadership is being seen as important in managing change, which in turn will make a significant contribution, at the interfaces of the curricular structure, to the department and the organization, and to the implementation of approaches such as problem-based learning. Problem-based learning too could be said to offer students opportunities to develop leadership abilities because of the way it encourages students to manage multiple meanings, and to develop strategies for critical action.

Curricular frameworks have shifted towards modularization in order to offer students more flexibility and choice, yet many undertaking education for the professions feel that it has created less of both and, at the same time, created a more fragmented curriculum than in former years. The curriculum may not actually be more fragmented. Curricula may have been disparate in former years but it might now be the case that modularization points up the fault lines in the structure since it tends to show up areas of disintegration more clearly than courses that were structured around a build-up of content. In some cases, however, problem-based learning in modular programmes can provide a holding mechanism to enable students to fuse knowledge and skills across modular boundaries as long as problem-based learning is seen as the core principle into which lectures, seminars and skills laboratory sessions feed. A further difficulty is the notion of a common course structure designed to offer students opportunities to choose other modules beyond their course, one which rarely works in practice. Students are offered the possibility of choice but not the reality. Requirements from professional bodies mean that students opting into and out of modules, for instance in health sciences, is not practicable. What tends to occur is that problem-based learning itself becomes modularized, only occurring in particular areas of the curriculum. Students then experience problem-based learning as an approach to learning that promotes integration of knowledge and abilities but only within given modules rather than necessarily across them. Dual qualification systems seem to have complicated this issue further. For example, the necessity of fulfilling the requirements of a professional qualification with clearly defined objectives, as well as the curriculum guidelines of the university, often results in curricula containing highly structured components, leaving students ill-equipped to organize their time during problem-based learning components of the course.

Information and Communication Technology (ICT) has far reaching implications for universities in general since the emphasis on technological learning is likely to increase as resources decrease. It will be argued by some that overuse of ICT will result in just high quality infotainment, but technological learning can offer students alternative choices for gaining knowledge and information. At the same time current trends and policies are promoting strong links between problem-based learning and ICT. For example, the Institute for Public Policy Research has established a pilot project at Ultralab at Anglia Polytechnic University. This project has been set up to examine the concept of an online learning network. What is significant about this project is that its initial premise was that 'online communities flourish when the participants are self-directed and participate in designing their learning' (Heppell and Ramondt, 1998: 8), which is also a central premise of many problem-based curricula. What is more, it is likely that with increases in student numbers the notion of problem-based learning groups in seminar rooms will become instead 'virtual learning communities' and furthermore research into such communities would suggest that there need not be a loss in the quality of the learning. In curricula where large student numbers mean more lectures, more problem-based learning 'large-group-style', and less seminars, virtual learning communities could in fact improve the quality and experience of learning for terrestrial courses, as well as solving some of the difficulties of small group work, such as the demand for rooms when dealing with cohorts of over 250 students.

Conclusion

The attractions of problem-based learning are many and thus the implementation of problem-based learning, in the UK at least, is becoming widespread; yet it is naive to assume that it is possible to adopt problem-based learning with ease. As yet there are few, if any, universities that see teaching and learning innovations such as problem-based learning from an holistic organizational perspective. Instead what tends to occur is that the innovators and innovations remain in isolation and perhaps only see the light of day when it suits the university to pull them out of the cupboard for all to see. The dangers of ignoring the impact of political and organizational issues on problem-based learning can be seen in the outright failure of those who have attempted to implement it whilst ignoring the organizational consequences. The introduction of problem-based learning will affect the staff at every level, whether overtly or covertly, within the organization. At the same time the organization will in turn affect the model of problem-based learning on offer, and the kinds of experiences students are likely to encounter or be able to create for themselves.

Epilogue

In this book I have explored ways in which students and teachers manage complex and diverse learning in the context of their lives. These untold stories, which emerged from research into problem-based learning, also have more general application, as does the framework of Dimensions of Learner Experience. For example, it is often assumed that students *have* a learning style and that they are particular *kinds* of thinkers. However, what has become apparent here is that although students in higher education may have particular preferences for particular types of learning, in fact students and the ways in which they learn are as individual as people and their circumstances. This may seem obvious, but there is still a tendency to want to categorize learners in over-simplistic ways that consequently deny the vitality of their learner identity. There is an inclination, too, to believe that problem-based learning can only work with mature students, students who are capable of high grades or alternatively students who have significant life experience. Yet it would seem that many of the difficulties which occur in curricula that use problem-based learning do not relate to what students bring with them to the particular course, but instead relate to what actually happens to them when they get there. Staff assumptions about what is valuable, along with the model of problem-based learning on offer, can disable students just as much as anything they feel they lack personally in relation to what they are expected to learn. What is also evident is that students are so diverse, in terms of the clientele in the higher education system, that it is not possible to point to particular types of students and thus suggest there would be those for whom problem-based learning particularly worked. However, students' own agenda and their reasons for 'being learners' at a particular point in their lives, can affect, to a large extent, their expectation of, and response to, the kinds of learning on offer and the model of problem-based learning with which they are expected to engage.

Revisiting the argument

The central argument of this book is that the potential and influence of problem-based learning is yet to be realized in the context of higher education. I have argued that problem-based learning is an important approach to learning that should be centrally located in higher education. Mistaken assumptions about problem-based learning have resulted in misunderstandings about the possibilities for its use in higher education. This, coupled with confusion about the relationship between problem-based learning and problem-solving, has meant that the value of problem-based learning has been underestimated in terms of the ways in which it can:

- equip students for the world of work
- offer students opportunities to learn how to learn
- help students develop independence in enquiry and the ability to contest and debate
- improve students' learning by helping them to learn with complexity and through ambiguity
- help students to realize and develop their learner identity
- enable students to see learning as a lifelong cyclical process through which to develop increasing understandings of themselves and the situations in which they learn effectively
- offer staff a means of responding to the problem of ever increasing pressures on curriculum content
- provide opportunities for teaching that are grounded in the world of work.

However, an area that requires further exploration is the 'lived curriculum'. Further studies that get to the heart of what occurs for staff and students in problem-based learning curricula are required. Although I have explored the impact of problem-based learning in people's lives in the context of four diverse curricula, there is still much work to be done in this field. While problem-based learning flourishes in the UK and elsewhere, the impact of such an exciting approach to learning on the text of people's lives remain largely undiscovered. Furthermore, there are still programmes being set up where important concerns raised here have not been discussed. For example, the important issues of learning context, learner identity and 'learning in relation' are rarely acknowledged or discussed when designing or implementing problem-based curricula. It is only by engaging with issues such as the organizational culture into which problem-based learning is placed, and the kind of model being offered, that it will be possible to bring to the fore the underlying agenda for adopting problem-based learning, which in turn can help students to understand the reasons for its implementation.

Realizing the potential of problem-based learning for higher education and for students can become a possibility through acknowledging that a number of forms of problem-based learning exist. Once this is acknowledged it will then be possible to make explicit the type of problem-based learning that is, or is intended to be, on offer and thus the different emphases and advantages will be explicit to the students, academe and to the world of work. Students will need to see that problem-based learning can offer them multiple opportunities for knowing and being in higher education. Admittedly this may not be possible unless staff can implement models of problem-based learning that are moving towards the ideals of Model V. These are ideals such as living and learning in the border country, creating communicative spaces and helping students to transcend and interrogate disciplinary boundaries through a commitment to exploring the subtext of those disciplines.

Problem-based learning for critical contestability offers us a means of breaching the chasms between professional education, and public and private sector. This is because problem-based learning of this sort both offers and demands that students, tutors and professionals in the field transcend the boundaries (set out in Figure 8.1) imposed through systems. In the context of Model V, learning outcomes may be defined in advance in order to satisfy professional and academic agenda. But for the staff and students involved in such problem-based learning programmes it should be possible to negotiate these and therefore offer students learning experiences that are seen and experienced as valuable to their identity construction. Thus, students will be helped to come to know that personal knowledge is as important as propositional knowledge and practical skills. They will begin to see that transcending frameworks; their own and those with which they are presented, will equip them to become effective practitioners for the future, more so than merely acquiring a sound body of knowledge or a set of narrow competencies. This may go some way to resolving some of the difficulties in current problem-based learning curricula where students repeat the same model of problem-based learning consistently through the whole programme and rarely, in reality, receive the opportunity to stretch themselves intellectually.

Perhaps though, I am too optimistic. It might be that problem-based learning, of the Model V variety, is not a complex enough model of learning to be able to encompass the needs of the learner heading towards becoming a future critical professional, with all the demands of a world characterized by incoherence and moving horizons. In fact it may be questioned, as Barnett (1997a) has done, whether higher education has, or will ever have, anything on offer that will facilitate the emergence of such a critical being. Whether it is in the demarcation of knowledge, in the representations of learning or in the view of the learner that characterize the distinction between these models, the key to understanding the complex nature of problem-based learning programmes centres on three areas. First, students' experiences, as documented in earlier chapters; second, the stances of those who have designed and who deliver the programme; and third, the influence of organizational structures and cultures on the problem-based learning (component of the) curriculum.

Moving along the edges of the end

As we move into an increasingly fragmented form of higher education what will become crucially important will be universities, of whatever genre, where the untold stories, not just of the students, but also of the staff and the managers, can be central to learning. We need to be asking of ourselves and of our organizations: 'how staff and students in higher education can be supported in generating and sustaining more interwoven positions, across institutions, disciplines, and new domains for knowledge generation; how we can begin to evolve and allow alternative understandings of "rigour" and "quality" that are more inclusive and respectful of diverse epistemological stances' (Weil, 1999: 172). As those involved in higher education we need to shape change rather than necessarily just respond to its effects. By addressing policies, mission statements, practices and strategies that have at their core the world of the learner, we can begin to talk about developing in students a kind of knowing that has authenticity, but at multiple levels and in diverse contexts. Yet the difficulty is still that knowledge generation in the contexts of students' lives rarely receives acknowledgment in the academe. The legitimacy of creating such knowledge is seen as questionable and the ways in which academic borders are controlled and patrolled means that the rites of passage over the borders are designed to maintain the *status quo*. Until there is space for creating kinds of legitimacy that allow for different ways of knowing then students, and staff new to, or wishing to challenge, the academe, will remain voiceless in the face of the silent dialogues and the hidden agenda of traditional practices. The hope lies deep within the complexities of the untold stories, through which it may be possible to help students of the future towards critical contestability.

Glossary

Complexity skills: the advanced skills that go beyond key skills and subject skills in a qualification framework, such as the capacity to work in complex and ambiguous contexts and to solve and manage problems in ways that transcend conventional lines of thinking.

Critical choice: the opportunity for students to examine their learner stances and to explore the pedagogic influences on the development of their learner identity.

Critical contestability: a position whereby students understand and acknowledge the transient nature of subject and discipline boundaries. They are able to transcend and interrogate these boundaries through a commitment to exploring the subtext of subjects and disciplines.

Dialogic learning: learning that occurs when insights and understandings emerge through dialogue in a learning environment. It is a form of learning where students draw on their own experience to explain the concepts and ideas with which they are presented, and then use that experience to make sense for themselves and also to explore further issues.

Disjunction: a sense of fragmentation of part of, or all of, the self, characterized by frustration and confusion and a loss of sense of self, which often results in anger and the need for right answers.

Domain: the overlapping spheres within each stance. The borders of the domains merge with one another and therefore shifts between domains are transitional areas where particular kinds of learning occur.

Interactional stance: the ways in which learners work and learn in groups and construct meaning in relation to one another.

Interprofessional education: the use of a variety of teaching methods and learning strategies to encourage interaction and interactive learning across the professions, which includes the development of skills and attitudes as well as knowledge.

Key skills: skills such as working with others, problem-solving and improving personal learning and performance that it is expected students will require for the world of work.

Learner identity: an identity formulated through the interaction of learner and learning. The notion of learner identity moves beyond, but encapsulates the notion of learning style, and encompasses positions that students take up in learning situations, whether consciously or unconsciously.

Learning context: the interplay of all the values, beliefs, relationships, frameworks and external structures that operate within a given learning environment.

Learning in relation: the ways in which students learn with and through others in such ways that they are helped to make connections between their lives, with other subjects and disciplines and with personal concerns. Learning in relation also incorporates not only the idea that students learn, as it were, in relation to their own knowledge and experience, but also to that of others.

Learner stances: the three stances (personal, pedagogical and interactional) that together form the framework of Dimensions of Learner Experience.

Pedagogical stance: the ways in which people see themselves as learners in particular educational environments.

Performative slide: the increasing focus in higher education on what students are able to *do*, which has emerged from the desire to equip students for life and work. Higher education is sliding towards encouraging students to perform rather than to necessarily critique and do.

Personal stance: the way in which staff and students see themselves in relation to the learning context and give their own distinctive meaning to their experience of that context.

Problem-solving learning: teaching where the focus is on students solving a given problem by acquiring the answers expected by the lecturer, answers that are rooted in the information supplied in some way to the students. The solutions are bounded by the content and students are expected to explore little extra material, other than that with which they have been provided, in order to discover the solutions.

Shared learning: any learning or teaching in which participants are drawn from two or more professional groups, which may include workshops and seminars as well as lectures.

Stance: one's attitude, belief or disposition towards a particular context, person or experience. It refers to a particular position one takes up in life towards something, at a particular point in time.

Transition: shifts in learner experience caused by a challenge to the person's lifeworld. Transitions occur in particular areas of students' lives, at different times and in distinct ways. The notion of transitions carries with it the idea of movement from one place to another and with it the necessity of taking up a new position in a different place.

Transitional learning: learning that occurs as a result of critical reflection on shifts (transitions) that have taken place for the students personally (including viscerally), pedagogically and/or interactionally.

References

Alavi, C. (1995) (ed.) *Problem-based Learning in a Health Sciences Curriculum*. London: Routledge.

Ausubel, D.P., Novak, J.S. and Hanesian, H. (1978) *Educational Psychology: A Cognitive View*. New York: Holt, Rinehart and Winston.

Association of University Teachers (AUT) (1995) *Higher Education – Preparing for the 21st Century*. London: Association of University Teachers.

Barnett, R. (1990) *The Idea of Higher Education*. Buckingham: Open University Press/SRHE.

Barnett, R. (1994) *The Limits of Competence*. Buckingham: Open University Press/SRHE.

Barnett, R. (1997a) *Higher Education: A Critical Business*. Buckingham: Open University Press/SRHE.

Barnett, R. (1997b) Realizing the University. Inaugural Professorial Lecture, Institute of Education, University of London, 25 November.

Barnett, R. (1998) What a performance: the changing patterns of undergraduate curricula. Keynote paper, Higher Education Close Up conference, University of Central Lancashire, 6–8 July.

Barnett, R.A., Becher, R.A. and Cork, N.M. (1987) Models of professional preparation: pharmacy, nursing and teacher education. *Studies in Higher Education*, 12(1): 51–63.

Barr, H. (1994) *Perspectives on Shared Learning*. London: CAIPE (Centre for the Advancement of Interprofessional Education).

Barrows, H.S. (1986) A taxonomy of problem-based learning methods. *Medical Education*, 20: 481–6.

Barrows, H.S. and Tamblyn, R.M. (1980) *Problem-based Learning, An Approach to Medical Education*. New York: Springer.

Beck, U. (1992) *Risk Society*. London: Sage.

Belenky, M.F., Clinchy, B.M., Goldberger, N.R. and Tarule, J.M. (1986) *Women's Ways of Knowing*. New York: Basic Books Inc.

Bennett, A. (1988) *Talking Heads*. London: BBC Books.

Bernstein, B. (1992) Pedagogic identities and educational reform. Paper given to Santiago conference, Cepal, 11 November, mimeo.

Bernstein, B. (1996) *Pedagogy, Symbolic Control and Identity*. London: Taylor & Francis.

Boud, D. (ed.) (1985) *Problem-based Learning in Education for the Professions*. Sydney: Higher Education Research and Development Society of Australasia.

Boud, D. (1989) Some competing traditions in experiential learning, in S. Weil and I. McGill (eds), *Making Sense of Experiential Learning: Diversity in Theory and Practice*. Buckingham: Open University Press/SRHE.

Boud, D. and Feletti, G. (eds) (1997) *The Challenge of Problem Based Learning*, 2nd edn. London: Kogan Page.

Boud, D., Keogh, R. and Walker, D. (eds) (1985) *Reflection: Turning Experience into Learning*. London: Kogan Page.

Boud, D., Cohen, R. and Walker, D. (1993) Introduction: understanding learning from experience, in D. Boud, R. Cohen and D. Walker (eds), *Using Experience for Learning*. Buckingham: Open University Press/SRHE.

Bridges, D. (1993) Transferable skills: a philosophical perspective. *Studies in Higher Education*, 18(1): 43–51.

Brookfield, S. (1985) A critical definition of adult education. *Adult Education Quarterly*, 36(1): 44–9.

Brookfield, S. (1994) Tales from the dark side: a phenomenography of adult critical reflection. *International Journal of Lifelong Education*, 13(3): 203–16

Cawley, P. (1997) A problem-based module in mechanical engineering, in D. Boud and G. Feletti (eds), *The Challenge of Problem Based Learning*, 2nd edn. London: Kogan Page.

Central Council for Education and Training in Social Work (CCETSW) (1989) *Requirements and Regulations for the Diploma in Social Work*, Paper 30. London: CCETSW.

Coles, C.R. (1985) Differences between conventional and problem-based curricula in their students' approaches to studying. *Medical Education*, 19: 308–9.

Deadman, A. (1998) Investigating the behind the scenes work in problem-based learning. Conference paper, Research in the Educational Context. NBS Teachers' conference, Aviemore, 26–7 February.

Dewey, J. (1938) *Experience and Education*. New York: Collier and Kappa Delta Pi.

Dolmans, D.H.J.M. and Schmidt, H.G. (1994) What drives the student in problem-based learning? *Medical Education*, 28(5): 372–80.

Drinan, J. (1991) The limits of problem-based learning, in D. Boud and G. Feletti (eds), *The Challenge of Problem Based Learning*. London: Kogan Page.

Eliot, T.S. (1954) *Selected Poetry*. London: Faber.

Engel, C. (1997) Not just a method but a way of learning, in D. Boud and G. Feletti (eds), *The Challenge of Problem Based Learning*. London: Kogan Page.

Entwistle, N.J. (1981) *Styles of Learning and Teaching*. New York: John Wiley and Sons.

Entwistle, N.J. (1987) A model of the teaching-learning process, in R.T.E. Richardson, M.W. Eysenck and D.W. Piper (eds), *Student Learning*. Buckingham: Open University Press/SRHE.

Eraut, M. (1985) Knowledge creation and knowledge in use in professional contexts. *Studies in Higher Education*, 10(2): 117–33.

Eraut, M. (1994) *Developing Professional Knowledge and Competence*. London: The Falmer Press.

Freire, P. (1972) *Pedagogy of the Oppressed*. London: Penguin Books.

Freire, P. (1974) *Education: The Practice of Freedom*. London: Writers and Readers Co-operative.

General Medical Council (1993) *Tomorrow's Doctors. Recommendations on Undergraduate Medical Education*. London: General Medical Council.

Gergen, K.J. (1987) Towards self as relationship, in K. Yardley and T. Honess (eds), *Self and Identity: Psychosocial Perspectives*. New York: John Wiley and Sons.

Gibbs, G. (1992) *Improving the Quality of Student Learning.* Bristol: Bristol Technical and Educational Services.

Giroux, H. (1992) *Border Crossings.* London: Routledge.

Glen, S. and Wilkie, K. (2000) *Problem-based Learning in Nursing.* London: Macmillan.

Griffiths, M. (1992) Autonomy and the fear of dependence. *Women's Studies International Forum,* 15(3): 351–62.

Habermas, J. (1989) *The Theory of Communicative Action, Vol. 2.* Cambridge: Polity.

Habermas, J. (1990) *Moral Consciousness and Communicative Action.* Cambridge: MIT Press.

Harley, P. and Lowe, S. (1998) Academics divided: The Research Assessment Exercise and the academic labour process. Conference paper, Higher Education Close Up conference, University of Central Lancashire, 6–8 July.

Havard, M., Hughes, M. and Clarke, J. (1998) The introduction and evaluation of key skills in undergraduate courses. *Journal of Further and Higher Education,* 22(1): 61–8.

Heppell, S. (1995) Children of the information age? A national survey of emergent capability. Ultralab/Apple Project. Anglia Polytechnic University. (available at: http://www.ultralab.anglia.ac.uk/pages/ultralab/Kids_Capabilities/)

Heppell, S. and Ramondt, L. (1998) Online learning – implications for the university for industry; a preliminary case study report. *Journal of Education through Partnership,* 2(2): 7–28.

Higgs, J. (1990) Fostering the acquisition of clinical reasoning skills. *New Zealand Journal of Physiotherapy,* December: 14–17.

Jansen, T. and Van Der Veen, R. (1992) Reflexive modernity, self-reflective biographies: adult education in the light of the risk society. *International Journal of Lifelong Education,* 11(4): 275–86.

Jarvis, P. (1987) *Adult Learning in the Social Context.* London: Croom Helm.

Johnson, R. (1988) 'Really useful knowledge': 1790–1850, in T. Lovett (ed.), *Radical Approaches to Adult Education: A Reader.* London: Routledge.

Knowles, M. (1978) *The Adult Learner: A Neglected Species.* Houston, TX: Gulf Publishing Company.

Kolb, D.A. and Fry, R. (1975) Towards an applied theory of experiential learning, in C.L. Cooper (ed.), *Theories of Group Processes.* Chichester: John Wiley and Sons.

Laurillard, D. (1979) The processes of student learning. *Higher Education,* 8: 395–409.

Laurillard, D. (1984) Learning from problem-solving, in F. Marton, D. Hounsell and N.J. Entwistle (eds), *The Experience of Learning.* Edinburgh: Scottish Academic Press.

Lukes, S. (1973) *Individualism.* Oxford: Basil Blackwell.

MacLure, M. and Marr, A. (1988) Teacher's jobs and lives: an interim report. Centre for Applied Research in Education, University of East Anglia, Norwich.

Margetson, D. (1991a) Is there a future for problem-based education? *Higher Education Review,* 23(2): 33–47.

Margetson, D. (1991b) Why is problem-based learning a challenge? in D. Boud and G. Feletti (eds), *The Challenge of Problem Based Learning.* London: Kogan Page.

Marton, F. and Säljö, R. (1976a) On qualitative differences in learning: I. Outcome and process. *British Journal of Educational Psychology,* 46: 4–11.

Marton, F. and Säljö, R. (1976b) On qualitative differences in learning: II. Outcome as a function of the learner's conception of the task. *British Journal of Educational Psychology,* 46: 115–27.

Marton, F. and Säljö, R. (1984) Approaches to learning, in F. Marton, D. Hounsell and N.J. Entwistle (eds), *The Experience of Learning*. Edinburgh: Scottish Academic Press.

Marton, F., Hounsell, D. and Entwistle, N.J. (eds) (1984) *The Experience of Learning*. Edinburgh: Scottish Academic Press.

McGuire, C.H. (1972) Research on identification of student needs. *Proceedings of the fourth Panamerican Conference on Medical Education*, Toronto, Canada.

McGuire, C.H. (1985) Medical problem solving: a critique of the literature. *Journal of Medical Education*, 60: 587–95.

McNay, I. (1995) From the collegial academy to corporate enterprise: The changing cultures of universities, in T. Schuller (ed.), *The Changing University?* Buckingham: Open University Press/SRHE.

Mennin, S.P. and Martinez-Burrola, N. (1990) The cost of problem-based vs. traditional medical education. *Medical Education*, 20(30): 187–94.

Mezirow, J. (1981) A critical theory of adult learning and education. *Adult Education*, 32: 3–24.

Middlehurst, R. (1995) Changing leadership in universities, in T. Schuller (ed.), *The Changing University?* Buckingham: Open University Press/SRHE.

Miller, C.M.L. and Parlett, M. (1974) *Up to the Mark: A Study of the Examination Game*. London: Society for Research into Higher Education.

National Committee of Inquiry into Higher Education (NCIHE) (1997) *Higher Education in the Learning Society* (Report of the National Committee of Inquiry into Higher Education chaired by Sir Ron Dearing). London: HMSO.

Neame, R.L.B. (1982) Academic roles and satisfaction in a problem-based medical curriculum. *Studies in Higher Education*, 7(2): 141–51.

Neisser, U. (1982) Memory: What are the important questions?, in U. Neisser (ed.), *Memory Observed: Remembering in Natural Contexts*. San Francisco: Freeman.

Niemi, H. and Kemmis, S. (1999) Communicative evaluation. *Lifelong Learning in Europe*, 4(1): 55–64.

Olesen, V.L. and Whittaker, E.W. (1968) *The Silent Dialogue*. London: Jossey-Bass.

Olson, J.O. (1987) The McMaster philosophy: a student's perspective on implementation. *Medical Education*, 21: 293–6.

O'Reilly, D. (1989) On being an educational fantasy engineer: incoherence, the individual and independent study, in S. Weil and I. McGill (eds), *Making Sense of Experiential Learning: Diversity in Theory and Practice*. Buckingham: Open University Press/SRHE.

Perry, W.G. (1970) *Forms of Intellectual and Ethical Development During the College Years: A Scheme*. New York: Holt, Rinehart and Winston.

Perry, W.G. (1981) Cognitive and ethical growth: the making of meaning, in A.W. Chickering (ed.), *The Modern American College: Responding to the New Realities of Diverse Students and a Changing Society*. San Francisco: Jossey-Bass.

Perry, W.G. (1988) 'Different worlds in the same classroom', in P. Ramsden (ed.), *Improving Learning. New Perspectives*. London: Kogan Page.

Piccone, P. (1981–82) Symposium: Intellectuals in the 1980s. *Telos*, 50: 115–60.

Polanyi, M. (1962) *Personal Knowledge: Towards a Post-Critical Philosophy*. London: Routledge and Kegan Paul.

Popper, K.R. (1970) Normal science and its dangers, in I. Lakatos and A. Musgrave (eds), *Criticisms and the Growth of Knowledge*. Cambridge: Cambridge University Press.

Ramsden. P. (1984) The context of learning, in F. Marton, D. Hounsell and N.J. Entwistle (eds), *The Experience of Learning*. Edinburgh: Scottish Academic Press.

Ramsden, P. (1992) *Learning to Teach in Higher Education.* London: Routledge.

Reason, P. and Rowan, J. (eds) (1981) *Human Inquiry – a Sourcebook of New Paradigm Research.* New York: John Wiley and Sons.

Robertson, D. (1998) What employers really really want: international competition for advanced skill capacity – some research evidence. Conference paper, Tomorrow's world: the globalisation of higher education conference, University of Lancaster, 16 December.

Rogers, C. (1969) *Freedom to Learn.* Columbus, OH: Merrill.

Ritzer, G. (1996) McUniversity in the postmodern consumer society. *Quality in Higher Education,* 2(3): 185–99.

Ryan, G. (1993) Student perceptions about self-directed learning in a professional course implementing problem-based learning. *Studies in Higher Education,* 18(1): 53–63.

Sadlo, G. (1994) Development of an Occupational Therapy Curriculum, Part 2: the BSc at the London School of Occupational Therapy. *British Journal of Occupational Therapy,* 57(3): 79–83.

Salmon, P. (1989) Personal stances in learning, in S. Weil and I. McGill (eds), *Making Sense of Experiential Learning.* Buckingham: Open University Press/SRHE.

Savin-Baden, M. (1996) Problem-based learning: a catalyst for enabling and disabling disjunction prompting transitions in learner stances?, unpublished PhD thesis. University of London Institute of Education.

Savin-Baden, M. (1998) Fugitives or nomads? The changing roles and relationships of staff and students in the context of global study. Conference paper, Tomorrow's world: the globalisation of higher education conference, University of Lancaster, 16 December.

Schumpeter, J. (1934) *The Theory of Economic Development.* Cambridge, MA: Harvard University Press.

Silver, H. (1998) Reinventing innovation. Conference paper, Managing Learning Innovation conference, University of Lincolnshire and Humberside, 1–2 September.

Silver, H., Hannan, A. and English, S. (1997) 'Innovation': questions of boundary, working paper no. 2. Faculty of Arts and Education, University of Plymouth.

Simon, W.E. (1996) The dumbing down of higher education. *The Wall Street Journal,* 19(March): A18.

Solzhenitsyn, A. (1988) *The First Circle.* London: Collins Harvill.

Taylor, I. (1997) *Developing Learning In Professional Education.* Buckingham: Open University Press/SRHE.

Taylor, I. and Burgess, H. (1995) Orientation to self-directed learning: paradox or paradigm. *Studies in Higher Education,* 20(1): 87–97.

Taylor, M. (1986) Learning for self-direction in the classroom: the pattern of a transition process. *Studies in Higher Education,* 11(1): 55–72.

Taylor, T., Gough, J., Bundrock, V. and Winter, R. (1998) A bleak outlook: academic staff perceptions of changes in core activities in Australian higher education, 1991–96. *Studies in Higher Education,* 23(3): 255–68.

Tennant, M. (1986) An evaluation of Knowles' Theory of Adult Learning. *International Journal of Lifelong Education,* 5(2): 113–22.

Terry, W. and Higgs, J. (1993) Educational programmes to develop clinical reasoning skills. *Australian Physiotherapy,* 39(1): 47–51.

Usher, R. and Edwards, R. (1994) *Postmodernism and Education.* London: Routledge.

Vernon, D.T.A and Blake, R.L. (1993) Does problem-based learning work? A meta-analysis of evaluative research. *Academic Medicine,* 68(7): 550–63.

Walton, H.J. and Mathews, M.B. (1989) Essentials of problem-based learning. *Medical Education*, 23: 542–58.

Weick, K. (1988) Educational organisations as loosely-coupled systems, in A. Westonby (ed.), *Cultures and Power in Educational Organizations*. Buckingham: Open University Press.

Weil, S. (1986) Non traditional learners within traditional higher education institutions: discovery and disappointment. *Studies in Higher Education*, 11(3): 219–35.

Weil, S. (1989) Access: Towards education or miseducation? Adults imagine the future, in O. Fulton (ed.), *Access and Institutional Change*. Buckingham: Open University Press/SRHE.

Weil, S. (1999) Recreating universities for 'beyond the stable state': from 'Dearingesque' systemic control to post-Dearing systemic learning and inquiry. *Journal of Systems Research and Behavioural Science*, 16(2): 171–90.

Wildemeersch, D. (1989) The principal meaning of dialogue for the construction and transformation of reality, in S. Weil and I. McGill (eds), *Making Sense of Experiential Learning: Diversity in Theory and Practice*. Buckingham: Open University Press/SRHE.

Williams, G. and Fry, H. (1994) *Longer Term Prospects for British Higher Education. A Report to the Committee of Vice-chancellors and Principals*. London: Institute of Education.

Index

Page numbers in **bold** indicate key references.

The Society for Research into Higher Education

The Society for Research into Higher Education (SRHE) exists to stimulate and coordinate research into all aspects of higher education. It aims to improve the quality of higher education through the encouragement of debate and publication on issues of policy, on the organization and management of higher education institutions, and on the curriculum, teaching and learning methods.

The Society is entirely independent and receives no subsidies, although individual events often receive sponsorship from business or industry. The society is financed through corporate and individual subscriptions and has members from many parts of the world.

Under the imprint *SRHE & Open University Press*, the Society is a specialist publisher of research, having over 80 titles in print. In addition to *SRHE News*, the society's newsletter, the society publishes three journals: *Studies in Higher Education* (three issues a year), *Higher Education Quarterly* and *Research into Higher Education Abstracts* (three issues a year).

The society runs frequent conferences, consultations, seminars and other events. The annual conference in December is organized at and with a higher education institution. There are a growing number of networks which focus on particular areas of interest, including:

Access	Learning Environment
Assessment	Legal Education
Consultants	Managing Innovation
Curriculum Development	New Technology for Learning
Eastern European	Postgraduate Issues
Educational Development Research	Quantitative Studies
FE/HE	Student Development
Funding	Vocational Qualifications
Graduate Employment	

Benefits to members

Individual

- The opportunity to participate in the Society's networks

- Reduced rates for the annual conferences
- Free copies of *Research into Higher Education Abstracts*
- Reduced rates for *Studies in Higher Education*
- Reduced rates for *Higher Education Quarterly*
- Free copy of *Register of Members' Research Interests* – includes valuable reference material on research being pursued by the Society's members
- Free copy of occasional in-house publications, e.g. *The Thirtieth Anniversary Seminars Presented by the Vice-Presidents*
- Free copies of *SRHE News* which informs members of the Society's activities and provides a calendar of events, with additional material provided in regular mailings
- A 35 per cent discount on all SRHE/Open University Press books
- Access to HESA statistics for student members
- The opportunity for you to apply for the annual research grants
- Inclusion of your research in the *Register of Members' Research Interests*

Corporate

- Reduced rates for the annual conferences
- The opportunity for members of the Institution to attend SRHE's network events at reduced rates
- Free copies of *Research into Higher Education Abstracts*
- Free copies of *Studies in Higher Education*
- Free copies of *Register of Members' Research Interests* – includes valuable reference material on research being pursued by the Society's members
- Free copy of occasional in-house publications
- Free copies of *SRHE News*
- A 35 per cent discount on all SRHE/Open University Press books
- Access to HESA statistics for research for students of the Institution
- The opportunity for members of the Institution to submit applications for the Society's research grants
- The opportunity to work with the Society and co-host conferences
- The opportunity to include in the *Register of Members' Research Interests* your Institution's research into aspects of higher education

Membership details: SRHE, 3 Devonshire Street, London
W1N 2BA, UK. Tel: 0171 637 2766. Fax: 0171 637 2781.
email: srhe@mailbox.ulcc.ac.uk
World Wide Web:http://www.srhe.ac.uk./srhe/
Catalogue: SRHE & Open University Press, Celtic Court,
22 Ballmoor, Buckingham MK18 1XW. Tel: 01280 823388.
Fax: 01280 823233. email: enquiries@openup.co.uk

SKILLS DEVELOPMENT IN HIGHER EDUCATION AND EMPLOYMENT

Neville Bennett, Elisabeth Dunne and Clive Carré

The last decade has seen radical changes in higher education. Long held assumptions about university and academic autonomy have been shattered as public and political interest in quality, standards and accountability have intensified efforts for reform. The increased influence of the state and employers in the curriculum of higher education is exemplified by the increasing emphasis on so-called core or transferable skills; an emphasis supported by the Dearing Report which identified what it called 'key' skills as necessary outcomes of all higher education programmes. However, there is little research evidence to support such assertions, or to underpin the identification of good practice in skill development in higher education or employment settings. Further, prescription has outrun the conceptualization of such skills; little attention has been paid to their theoretical underpinnings and definitions, or to assumptions concerning their transfer.

Thus the study reported in this book sets out to gain enhanced understandings of skill acquisition in higher education and employment settings with the aim of informing and improving provision. The findings and analyses provide a clear conceptualization of core and generic skills, and models of good practice in their delivery, derived from initiatives by employers and staff in higher education. Student and graduate employee perspectives on skill delivery and acquisition are presented, together with a clearer understanding of the influence of contexts in skill definition and use in workplace settings. Finally, important questions are raised about institutional influences and constraints on effective innovation, and the role that generic or key skills play in traditional academic study, and in workplace effectiveness.

Contents

Generic skills in the learning society – A conceptualization of skills and course provision – Beliefs and conceptions of teachers in higher education – The practices of university teachers – Student perspectives on skill development – Employer initiatives in higher education – Employers' perspectives on skills and their development – The graduate experience of work – The challenges of implementing generic skills – Appendices – References – Indexes.

c.208pp   0 335 20335 3 (Paperback)   0 335 20336 1 (Hardback)

USING EXPERIENCE FOR LEARNING

David Boud, Ruth Cohen and David Walker (eds)

This book is about the struggle to make sense of learning from experience. What are the key ideas that underpin learning from experience? How do we learn from experience? How does context and purpose influence learning? How does experience impact on individual and group learning? How can we help others to learn from their experience?

Using Experience for Learning reflects current interest in the importance of experience in informal and formal learning, whether it be applied for course credit, new forms of learning in the workplace, or acknowledging autonomous learning outside educational institutions. It also emphasizes the role of personal experience in learning: ideas are not separate from experience; relationships and personal interests impact on learning; and emotions have a vital part to play in intellectual learning. All the contributors write themselves into their chapters, giving an autobiographical account of how their experiences have influenced their learning and what has led them to their current views and practice.

Using Experience for Learning brings together a wide range of perspectives and conceptual frameworks with contributors from four continents, and is a valuable addition to the field of experiential learning.

Contents
Introduction: understanding learning from experience – Part 1: Introduction – Through the lens of learning: how the visceral experience of learning reframes teaching – Putting the heart back into learning – Activating internal processes in experiential learning – On becoming a maker of teachers: journey down a long hall of mirrors – Part 2: Introduction – Barriers to reflection on experience – Unlearning through experience – Experiential learning at a distance – Learning from experience in mathematics – Part 3: Introduction – How the T-Group changed my life: a sociological perspective on experiential group work – Living the learning: internalizing our model of group learning – Experiential learning and social transformation for a post-apartheid learning future – Experiential learning or learning from experience: does it make a difference? – Index.

Contributors
Lee Andresen, David Boud, Angela Brew, Stephen Brookfield, Ruth Cohen, Costas Criticos, Kathleen Dechant, Elizabeth Kasl, Victoria Marsick, John Mason, Nod Miller, John Mulligan, Denis Postle, Mary Thorpe, Robin Usher, David Walker.

208pp   0 335 19095 2 (Paperback)

DEVELOPING LEARNING IN PROFESSIONAL EDUCATION
PARTNERSHIPS FOR PRACTICE

Imogen Taylor

This is a timely addition to the literature which provides a challenge to professional education: both through its portrayal of a highly innovative problem-based course (and the rich detail of students' experience) which shows how a learner-centred approach can impact on participants; and through its location in much wider contexts of teaching and learning in professional education and in debates about the relationship between university education and professional practice.

Professor David Boud

At a time when attention is being directed increasingly towards lifelong learning, this book offers an extremely timely guide to the development of the learning skills needed to make this a reality. Readable, relevant and full of practical illustrations, it will be widely read by educators in a variety of professional contexts.

Professor Patricia Broadfoot

This book is about professional education and developing the required knowledge and skills to equip students for the pressing needs of professional practice. Student professionals from health care, teaching, business, law and social work must learn how to practise both independently (to respond to a constantly changing environment) and collaboratively (to respond to the complexity of today's society); also they must learn how to work in partnership with the consumers of professional services. Imogen Taylor explores how professional education can develop approaches to teaching and learning which both help learners to be reflexive, self-monitoring practitioners and meet the requirements of professional accrediting bodies. She draws upon her own research into students experiencing professional education based on small group, problem-based learning; on an extensive range of relevant international theory and research; and on her own long experience in professional education, training and practice.

This is an important resource for all those educators and trainers in professional education seeking to improve their own practice.

Contents

Part 1: Setting the scene – Introduction – Uneasy partnerships? – Part 2: Beginning learning – Transitions: traditional expectations and non-traditional courses – The personal is professional: using pre-course experience for learning – Part 3: The learning infrastructure – Learning for teamwork – Facilitating independent and interdependent learning – Restraint, resourcefulness and problem-based learning – Assessment: the crux of the matter – Part 4: Promising outcomes – Non-traditional learners: valuing diversity – Perspectives on education as preparation for practice – Partnerships with users of professional services – Appendix: enquiry and action learning (the structure) – References – Index.

224pp   0 335 19497 4 (Paperback)   0 335 19498 2 (Hardback)